CORPORATE CAPITAL

Control, Ownership, Saving and Crisis

CHRISTOS PITELIS

Department of Industrial Economics
University of Nottingham

The right of the University of Cambridge to print and sell all manner of books was granted by Henry VIII in 1534. The University has printed and published continuously since 1584.

CAMBRIDGE UNIVERSITY PRESS

Cambridge
London   New York   New Rochelle
Melbourne   Sydney

PUBLISHED BY THE PRESS SYNDICATE OF THE UNIVERSITY OF CAMBRIDGE
The Pitt Building, Trumpington Street, Cambridge, United Kingdom

CAMBRIDGE UNIVERSITY PRESS
The Edinburgh Building, Cambridge CB2 2RU, UK
40 West 20th Street, New York NY 10011–4211, USA
477 Williamstown Road, Port Melbourne, VIC 3207, Australia
Ruiz de Alarcón 13, 28014 Madrid, Spain
Dock House, The Waterfront, Cape Town 8001, South Africa

http://www.cambridge.org

First published 1987
First paperback edition 2004

A catalogue record for this book is available from the British Library

Library of Congress cataloguing in publication data

Pitelis, Christos.
Corporate capital.
Bibliography.
Includes index.
1. Corporations – Finance. 2. Capital investments.
I. Title.
HG4026.P575 1987   658.1´5   86-26807

ISBN 0 521 32848 9 hardback
ISBN 0 521 60745 0 paperback

CORPORATE CAPITAL

Ελένη

Contents

Acknowledgements

The basic ideas developed in this monograph were conceived in the 1982–84 period, during which I worked for a PhD thesis at the Economics Department, University of Warwick, under the supervision of Keith Cowling. Our discussions, his comments and his book *Monopoly Capitalism* have had a dramatic influence on my thought, evident I believe in the pages of the present monograph. During the writing of my thesis, and in the one and a half years following its completion, a number of papers based on it were presented at a number of conferences, seminars, and workshops and were published in various economics journals. The comments and discussions I received from the participants and referees of the papers helped me extend my arguments and improve their weaknesses to such an extent that (parts of) the present monograph now bear only remote resemblance to the original thesis. Numerous people also gave me comments on individual papers, later extended to chapters of the present work. I grasp the opportunity to extend my gratitude to them all.

I am particularly indebted to Roger Sugden. His work, comments, and our discussions and joint work during the last five years have proved a continuous source of encouragement and inspiration. He also read thoroughly the whole typescript and gave me his final detailed comments and corrections. I also want to give special mention to Malcolm Sawyer. In a number of capacities, external examiner, conference chairperson, and referee of the proposal of this monograph, he offered me invaluable help towards improving some of its substantive and presentational aspects. Francis Brooke's editorial interest and the encouragement he gave to extensions of the original thesis helped considerably in shaping the final product. I am also grateful for Iain White's help with the sub-editing. For research assistance I am indebted to Helen Whalley. For efficient and speedy typing to Rosemary Reid. My wife, Ioanna, is one of two parties in the absence of which this work might never have been realized; the other is the Greek State Scholarships Foundation which financed my postgraduate studies at Warwick.

May 1986   CHRISTOS PITELIS

CHAPTER 1

The socialization of corporate ownership

This book aims at examining the impact of the emergence and growth of the modern corporation – the joint stock company (hereafter JSC) – on advanced capitalist economies, in particular on corporate control and shareownership, consumers' choice, the mobilization of financial capital and the saving function, and capitalism's potential inherent tendency towards stagnation and crisis.[1]

The principal feature of the modern corporation is that, unlike its predecessor – the small nineteenth-century firm – it is not owned by an individual tycoon or family but rather by the public at large through shareholding.[2] The result of the historical emergence and dilution of shareownership is a tendency towards the socialization of corporate ownership (hereafter SOCO), or equivalently a tendency towards the *socialization of the ownership of the means of production* (hereafter SOMP) in advanced capitalist countries.

In this book, I identify two stages in the above tendency. First, direct or voluntary shareholding, i.e. the direct purchase of corporate shares by those households willing and able to do so. Second, indirect, often compulsory, shareholding. This is mainly associated with the so-called pension funds revolution, i.e. the introduction and expansion of compulsory funded occupational pension fund schemes. The role of such schemes is to 'defer' a part of the wage earners' income in order to finance their future retirement. In the meantime the income of the funds is invested by those who control them, mainly industrial firms or financial institutions, in the purchase of corporate shares, government securities, etc., at home or overseas. This renders the participants to the pension fund the ultimate beneficiaries ('owners') of corporate shares. Thus, the pension funds 'revolution' tends to extend the tendency towards SOMP to sections of the population which in the absence of the pension fund might not have decided voluntarily to purchase shares.[3]

The emergence of the joint-stock company (JSC) and its associated tendency towards SOMP mark a new era in the development of capitalism. Previously, capitalism was characterized by an important antithesis; the coexistence of *social production*, the participation of the vast majority of people in the production process, and *private appropriation*, i.e. the appropriation of (a disproportionate part of) the social product by a minority of people who owned and controlled the means of production.

The tendency towards SOMP, I suggest, raises the above antithesis to its highest level; as it results in a coexistence of *social ownership*, with *social production* on the one hand, and *private appropriation* on the other. A small minority of people is now appropriating the social product by virtue of their control over the means of production, the largest part of which is owned collectively by others.

The tendency towards SOMP has important implications for the analysis of the behaviour of advanced capitalist countries. First, in the earlier phase of capitalist development, firms were owned and controlled by an individual tycoon or a family of capitalists. The dilution of corporate ownership tends to separate (parts of) corporate ownership from the unity ownership *and* control, and raises the important question: who exercises effective control over today's giant corporations? Second, and related to the above, is the issue of shareholder ('social') choice. Unless corporate control is exercised collectively by all owners, corporate policies may diverge from the desires of some (non-controlling) shareholders. Decisions, for example, on corporate retained earnings and pension funds may constrain shareholders' choice over their consumption/saving by reducing their disposable income. In its turn this may affect the ability of the corporate sector as a whole to increase financial capital accumulation (aggregate savings). All of this will be reflected in the form of the saving function. Finally, the dilution of shareholding will tend to raise the proportion of the income of the private (personal plus corporate) sector controlled by the corporate sector. This will tend to reduce the part of private income available for consumption, and thus may sow the seeds of a realization crisis, i.e. a situation where produced goods cannot be sold at a profitable price. This will tend to induce a stagnationist tendency in advanced capitalist economies, inherent in them to the same extent as the JSC and the tendency towards SOMP.

The above questions will be analysed in the next four chapters. Chapter 2 will examine the impact of the tendency towards SOMP on the issue of corporate control, focussing in particular on the notion of an alleged separation of ownership from control. Three competing approaches to the issue of corporate control will be identified; the neoclassical, the managerialist and the Marxist.[4] According to the first, effective corporate control is exercised by *all* shareholders. The dilution of corporate ownership simply results in a higher proportion of people owning and controlling a society's corporations. For the managerialists, on the other hand, the degree of today's dilution of corporate ownership raises doubts about the alleged ability of (any) owners to exercise effective corporate control. Instead, the dilution of corporate ownership tends to result in a post-capitalist society where *no* individual shareholder can exercise control by virtue of the very small shareholdings. Actual control is assumed to pass to the professional management of the corporations, thus the term 'managerialism'. Finally, many Marxists have accepted the idea of a 'managerial revolution'. They argued, however, that its emergence has not resulted in any qualitative changes in the nature of capitalism. The structure of the capitalist system is still such as to ensure that (high level) managers will tend to be recruited from the ranks of the big shareholders (capitalists) and/or behave as if they were themselves capitalists, i.e. strive for high profits.

The problem with all the above approaches, I suggest, is that they do not derive their conclusions from a coherent analysis of the effects over time of the expansion of firms on shareownership and control. They are static and ahistorical in that they attempt to infer the nature of control today in the light of current (dispersed) ownership. Instead, this book starts from the indisputable fact of the combination of ownership *and* control in the hands of individual capitalists in the small firms that were the predecessors of the JSCs, and examines the impact of the expansionist policies of these capitalists on shareownership and control. In doing to, I suggest that the idea of the managerialist revolution is arbitrary, implausible and, perhaps more importantly, inconsistent with its own focus on individual utility maximization. In a historical sense, the selling of shares has been the (conscious) decision of the controlling capitalists to expand their firms and further their interests. Assuming that capitalists are rational, utility-maximizing individuals in the neoclassical/managerialist sense, it follows that, in expanding their firms, capitalists will wish to retain control. Capitalists will only lose control if they decide to do so, or if they cannot expand *and* retain control.

That capitalists will find it more beneficial to relinquish control is not self-evident and has not been demonstrated. That capitalists cannot expand and retain control appears implausible, given that in an *ex-ante* sense both the decision to sell shares and the extent to which shares are sold are the capitalists' own decisions. The decision to appoint a (new) manager is similar. Given that, I suggest, my analysis leads smoothly to the theoretical conclusion that the modern corporation of today is controlled by a group of big shareholders and high-level managers (capitalists) who exercise this control *via* only partial ownership. Observed shareholdings should, as a result, be considered sufficient to ensure control by a collusive subset of capitalists in every specific case. This inverts the underlying chain of causality in the managerialist argument which runs from assumptions on *ad-hoc* shareholding percentages necessary for control, to control itself. Our analysis starts from the unity of ownership and control and examines the potential effects of firms' expansion on control and ownership. An analysis of the existing direct and indirect evidence appears to lend support to the view given here.

Related to the question of corporate control is the potential impact of the location of control on shareholders' choices over their desired consumption/saving patterns and thus on financial capital accumulation. I examine this question in chapter 3. The neoclassical view on this issue is that there is no link between corporate control and shareholders' consumption/saving patterns, because the shareholders as a whole are in effective control of firms. Even if corporate policies diverge from consumers' preferences, moreover, rational individuals will realize this and react appropriately so as to offset the impact of undesired corporate policies. In the case, for example, of corporate saving, the above implies that in shareholders' minds personal saving and corporate saving are perfect substitutes, i.e. different types of household saving. Corporate saving policies as a result do not constrain the consumption/saving patterns of households; what we have here is a harmony view.

The neoclassical view is challenged by the managerialists. In their view, managers control the firms and maximize a utility function different from the shareholders'. The latter wish to consume as much as they can – partly as a result of the advertising and other selling–promotion policies of the large firms – and thus favour high dividends and low retentions. Managers, on the other hand, favour high growth and high retention ratios. Shareholders' ability to thwart managers' decisions is limited, partly because they lack full information about managers' actions, but also due to the favourable tax treatment of retentions and as a result of imperfections in capital markets and the associated liquidity constraints on shareholders. In apparent contrast to the neoclassical view, managerialists conclude that all shareholders' choices are constrained by the decisions of non-shareholder managers, who thus become the *sine qua non* of the continuation of the process of capital accumulation under advanced capitalism. This managerialist view is also echoed in the writings of some Marxists.

Building upon chapters 1–2, I suggest in chapter 3 that the above approaches capture only parts of the reality, and fail to provide a comprehensive analysis of the issue. In particular I suggest that the choices of the controlling capitalists are not constrained by corporate decisions, as it is they themselves who take these decisions. In this sense the neoclassical hypothesis is a good description of capitalists' behaviour.

Capitalists' decisions, however, may constrain the choices of the non-controlling shareholders, partly for the reasons advanced by the managerialists. In this sense the latters' analysis is a good description of non-controlling shareholders' behaviour. Overall, the extent to which financial capital accumulation will increase following increases in corporate saving will depend upon the proportion of total shareholding owned by the capitalists and the ability of non-controlling shareholders to influence corporate policy.

An important reason why non-controlling shareholders may fail fully to offset the effect of corporate saving policies on their consumption/saving is the 'pension funds revolution'. This has resulted in a sizeable proportion of corporate shares being owned by people, usually wage earners, who have no control over or even knowledge of their ownership claims on shares bought by 'their' funds. This makes it unlikely that these indirect shareholders will react, e.g. to increases in corporate retentions by reducing their saving, or by borrowing and/or trying to 'declare their dividends', i.e. to sell 'their' shares. In this sense, the 'pension funds revolution' helps to maintain and perhaps enhance the aggregate level of shareholding, and removes from the non-controlling shareholders their ultimate means of putting pressure on corporate controllers; their ability to sell and/or not to add further to their shareholding. In addition, through their net inflow (the difference between contributions to, and benefits paid by, the pension funds) the 'pension funds revolution' results in another source of corporate saving – changes in which may further affect financial capital accumulation by constraining wage earners' consumption/saving choices.

A detailed analysis of the existing direct and indirect evidence on the substitutability between corporate and personal saving appears to lend support to the proposition that such substitutability may not be perfect. The reason for the potential existence of differential 'preferences' on the retention and net inflow into pension-funds' ratios between capitalists and non-controlling shareholders, I suggest, is to be found in capitalists' needs to accumulate profits and realize them, i.e. be able to sell produced goods at a profitable price. The need to accumulate profits arises from the pressures on firms to compete successfully with rivals so as to survive. This necessitates the retention of profits for expansion, and thus explains capitalists' 'preference' for high retentions. The need, however, to sell products necessitates an attempt to boost consumption through advertising and other such policies. The latter tend to ensure a low 'preference' for retention by the non-controlling shareholders. Overall, the competition-driven capitalist need to accumulate ensures the endogeneity to the system of capitalists' 'preferences' as well as the non-controlling shareholders' 'preferences'; all of which casts doubt on the neoclassical assumption of consumer sovereignty.

The potential impact of the tendency towards SOMP on the (non-controlling) shareholders' choices over their consumption/saving has been formalized in the theory of the saving function; this issue is taken up in chapter 4. In the tradition of the classical economists, for example, it was suggested that all saving is made out of profits, while workers do not save, basically because of their subsistence requirements. In a more recent version of this thesis, workers are 'allowed' to save but the 'propensity' to save from wages is lower than from profits. For the proponents of this view, the so-called neo-Keynesians, the dilution of shareownership and its associated retention of profit within the corporation is an important reason for the existence of such differential saving propensities between different types of household income.

If corporate retention is the main reason for the existence of a higher 'propensity' to save profits, one may shift one's emphasis from differential 'propensities' between different types of household income, to differential propensities between household income as a whole on the one hand, and corporate income on the other. This shift in emphasis is in line with the theorizing of a wide spectrum of economic ideologies: the managerialists, the post-Keynesians and the Marxists. The saving function formalizing the above ideas has been named the 'managerialist saving function' (MSF).

In its present form the MSF fails to account for the existence of indirect shareholding through wage earners' pension funds, and it needs to be developed in this direction. According to the amended MSF, households save only out of their discretionary disposable income shares, i.e. net of both corporate retentions and the net inflow into pension funds. The last two, on the other hand, represent total corporate saving. The MSF and its developed version proposed in this chapter are not necessarily the product of the existence of a 'managerial revolution'. Rather they are the result of the coexistence of social ownership and minority control in today's corporations. In this sense the MSF and its extension are the product of a stage in capitalist development characterized by the existence of JSCs. As this stage may be referred to as Corporate Capitalism, we name our proposed extension of the MSF here, the Corporate Capitalism Saving Function (CCSF).

Both the MSF and the CCSF assume implicitly that corporate retentions and pension funds are not perfect substitutes for discretionary personal saving. In this sense they are in stark contrast to the neoclassical views on this issue. Although there is no independent direct evidence to test the

CCSF, three types of indirect evidence have implications for it. First, studies on the substitutability between corporate retentions, pension funds, and personal saving. Second, studies on the existence of differential saving propensities between different types of household income. Third, tests of the 'Galbraith–Marglin' hypothesis, that the propensity to save discretionary household income is zero. A detailed survey of the existing evidence on the above is found to lend support to the CCSF.

A problem with the above evidence is that it has been derived by making use of often differing specifications of the consumption/saving function, different data sets and periods covered and different definitions of the income and saving variables. This necessitates the testing of the above hypotheses in a common, coherent framework free from the above limitations. To do this, I first show that the estimated forms of most existing theories of the consumption/saving function, the Life Cycle Hypothesis (LCH), the Houthakker–Taylor (H–T) model, the Adaptive Expectations/Permanent Income (AE/PI) Hypothesis, the 'Error Correction' (EC) model and the Simple Lag/Habit Persistence (SL/HP) Hypothesis, lead to a common 'general' estimated form of the saving function. The latter can then, I believe, be used as a framework for testing all the hypotheses/saving functions discussed so far. This we do by defining household saving and income net of corporate retentions and pension funds in line with my analysis so far, and then extending the above 'general' framework to include retentions and pension funds as additional explanatory variables.

The econometric methodology adopted is the 'general to specific', i.e. we start from the most unrestricted estimated equation consistent with our theoretical model, and then we test it down to obtain the equation that 'explains' the data generation process most parsimoniously. The results obtained by using postwar, 1952–84, UK data lend support to our theoretical propositions. In particular it is found that (non-controlling) households do not (fully) account for their ownership claims on income they do not control when making their consumption/saving decisions. The Galbraith–Marglin hypothesis, moreover, appears to be supported by the data, in that households are found to save only out of their changes in income. The implication of the above is that corporate retentions and pension funds account for virtually all financial capital accumulation in the economy, and that no differential saving 'propensities' appear to exist out of (non-controlling) households' discretionary wage and profit types of income. It is finally found that the neo-Keynesian saving function and the MSF can be obtained from the CCSF by imposing on it what have already been found to be invalid restrictions: i.e. equal 'propensities' to save from net wage income and pension funds and/or net profit income and corporate retentions. This casts doubt on the conventional use of the term 'propensity'. Far from representing 'propensities' the thus-obtained proportions of (types of) income saved are actually an amalgam of actual propensities (out of households' discretionary income shares), corporate saving and potentially transient saving due to households' changes in incomes. The term 'propensity' is misleading in that it conveys the impression that all households can act in accord to their 'psychological' urges, i.e. that they are sovereign.[5]

At the aggregate level the tendency towards SOMP will tend to result in an increasingly higher proportion of private income being controlled by the corporate sector, i.e. an increasingly lower proportion being available to households for consumption. This introduces an underconsumptionist tendency in advanced capitalist economies, a situation where consumers' expenditure is insufficient to buy the full-capacity consumption-goods product of the corporate sector. Such a situation contains the seeds of a realization crisis, a situation in which the total effective demand of the private sector (consumption plus investment) is insufficient to absorb the full-capacity product of the corporate sector. As a result firms cannot sell their products at a profitable price, i.e. fail to realize their potential profits.

The above scenario is examined in chapter 5. It is suggested in particular that the tendency towards SOMP will tend to increase the share of profits and reduce the share of consumption in private disposable income. Faced with reduced demand for their products, firms producing consumption-goods may react by cutting back their output and their demand for the products of the capital-goods firms. The overall effect may be to increase excess capacity in the economy as a whole. Restrictions on output and increases in excess capacity may in their turn adversely affect the ratio of profits to capital stock and private investment, giving rise to a tendency towards a realization crisis.

It is widely believed that the profit rate is an important determinant of investment. The rate of profit can be decomposed into three constituent parts. The rate of capacity utilization, the profit share, and the productivity of capital. Our analysis suggests that the tendency towards SOMP will tend to reduce capacity utilization, and increase the profit share. It has no implications for the productivity of capital. Although increases in the share of profits will tend to exert a positive impact on the profit rate and investment, the impact of declining consumption on capacity utilization will tend to offset this positive effect, thus putting definite limits on increases in profit-rates and investment. As a result increases in investment will tend to be insufficient to compensate for reductions in consumption, thereby failing to offset the tendency towards realization crisis.

The above tendency will tend to be reinforced if the productivity of capital declines, as a result, for example, of increases in the organic composition of capital (the ratio of constant capital – machinery – to variable capital – labour), leading to a decline in the rate of profit and investment. This possibility is consistent with the Marxist 'law' of the declining rate of profit, due to a rising organic composition of capital resulting from labour-saving technological change. It brings together in a common framework the Marxist views on underconsumption and the declining rate of profit. In the above scenario the crisis will tend to manifest itself in terms of an increasing proportion of private income not being consumed or invested ('excess saving'), increasing excess-capacity rates, and their associated pressures on the profitability of firms. The conjunction of these latter, on the other hand, may induce firms to look for overseas markets. In this sense, we can see the internationalization of production as the result of the effects of the tendency towards SOMP on the effective demand and profitability of the domestic economies of advanced capitalist countries.

In the above analysis, the source of the realization crisis is an increase in the ratio of corporate income (and saving) to private income, not fully offset by reductions in the personal saving rate. In this sense, it is in stark contrast to the neoclassical view, according to which a secular decline in the consumption share cannot arise without changes in (the determinants of) consumers' preferences. It can accommodate, however, the Keynesian and Marxist views on underconsumption. According to the former, under the assumption of a higher 'propensity' to save profits, an underconsumptionist tendency may arise if changes take place redistributing income from wages to profits. In the Marxist tradition, on the other hand, the ability of giant firms to increase profit margins through time by cutting marginal costs and/or passing on increases in marginal costs to consumers by increasing prices, results in a tendency for the 'surplus' to rise, i.e. for total profits plus the wasteful expenditures of the corporate and the state sectors to rise. This tends to reduce the shares of consumption and investment in national product, thus leading to a realization crisis.

Our discussion and evidence casts doubt on the neoclassical thesis. Although our analysis can be cast in terms of differential wage and profit income propensities and/or increasing profit shares (approximations to the 'surplus'), it is more general in that it fully accounts for the role of retained wage income (net inflow into pension funds), provides an explanation as to why changes in income distribution occur over time and does not require conscious attempts on the part of the firms to increase the 'surplus' for an underconsumptionist tendency to operate. More generally, while our scenario incorporates the main concerns of earlier underconsumptionist theories – (increasing) inequalities in income distribution, and thus increasing profit shares and 'excess saving' – it regards all the above as being the result rather than the cause of the crisis. It is the need to accumulate profits that leads to the tendency towards SOMP and thus gradually creates the very conditions that ensure a brake on its continuation.

In a closed economy, the tendency towards SOMP, in spite of its long-run consequences for effective demand, can be explained in terms of the 'anarchy' of the capitalist system, i.e. the fact that individual firms pursue their own interests without necessarily considering the overall macroeconomic effects of their policies. Thus in the closed economy the crisis appears to be the result of domestic capitalist policies. Its emergence is also bound to defeat the very need for SOMP, and thus put a (temporary) end to it.

The above need not be the case in the presence of internationalized production. The ability of firms to export and/or produce directly overseas may tend to induce firms to carry on the tendency towards SOMP at the domestic level in advanced capitalist countries for as long as the potential for domestic saving and profitable outlets abroad are available. This may tend to prolong a realization crisis domestically. The degree and nature of the international activities of a country's capital, moreover, may be a factor in explaining the relative performance of this country in the crisis.

A number of counterforces exist, often believed to mitigate a realization crisis; advertising and Research and Development policies of firms, as well as conscious policies by the state intended to stabilize and/or expand the economy. Still, we suggest, their effects are not straightforward or unidirectional. The ability of the state in particular to combat the crisis unilaterally in an international setting is continually decreasing. A reason for this is the increasing bargaining power of the transnational corporations that arises from the locational flexibility of their operations. This may tend to reduce the economic role of the capitalist states to the provision of a satisfactory environment for domestic investment of internationally oriented domestic or overseas capital, and the maintenance of a police and military force capable of ensuring the protection of capital's interests domestically and/or overseas. The ability of international capital to finance its operations partly by internationalizing the tendency towards SOMP may gradually result in a globalization of the tendency towards realization crisis and stagnation.

The above suggestions appear to be in line with the existing evidence in the US and the UK, providing a partial explanation for the recent prolonged recession in these countries and the so-called 'relative decline' of the UK. A fuller explanation is obtained when our suggestions are complemented by those of other existing theories on crisis and the 'relative decline'.

CHAPTER 2

Corporate control, corporate ownership

The emergence of the joint stock company and its associated tendency towards the socialization of the ownership of the means of production (SOMP) has raised the question: who controls these companies? Unlike their predecessors, the small nineteenth-century firms, which were owned and controlled often by one individual or a family, the joint stock companies are 'owned' by the public at large. In view of the often wide dispersal of shareholding, the distinct possibility emerges that not all shareholders will exercise corporate control. In this sense the very existence of the joint stock company implies a potential separation of ownership from the unity of ownership *and* control.

The above does not necessarily imply a separation of ownership from control. Control can be in the hands of the shareholders as a whole, a subset of the shareholders or no shareholders at all, in which case control may be exercised by a group of non-shareholders, e.g. professional managers and/or technical experts. It is only in this last case that ownership and control are divorced. In the first case ownership and control are still a unity, while in the second only a subset of owners is separated from control, i.e. a partial separation of ownership from control exists.

Consistent with their focus on 'consumer sovereignty', orthodox neoclassical economists largely ignored the possibility of the separation of ownership from the unity of ownership *and* control. According to their often implicit view, all shareholders are in control of firms. This control effectively lies in the ability of the shareholders to sell their shares and possibly move to another company whose policies are closer to their preferences. In doing so all shareholders ensure that the companies they 'own' are pursuing policies in line with their preferences. In this sense corporate policies are the result of a global consensus and thus all shareholders are in control of firms.

The possibility that shareholders no longer control firms and that control is now exercised by professional managers has forcefully been advanced by the so-called managerialist school. In essence the managerialist argument is that dispersal of shareholding implies that eventually no shareholder will have sufficient shares to exercise control. In default of owners' control the latter will now be with the professional managers of the firms. Assuming that a certain percentage of shares is required in order to exercise control, firms can be classified as manager or owner controlled by observing whether in any particular firm there is a cohesive group of shareholders which possesses more than the assumed share percentage. If such a group is found, the firm is said to be owner-controlled. If not, manager-controlled.

The possibility that some firms may be controlled by managers also raises the question of the aims that managers pursue. To the extent that the latter differ from those of the owners, profit maximization may no longer be *the* aim of corporations. Instead managers may sacrifice some profits in order to pursue aims that suit better their own interests.

The implications of the managerialist 'revolution' have been questioned by authors in the Marxist tradition. If a capitalist class, which owns and controls the means of production, can still be identified today, then the managers can only be capitalists themselves, or functionaries of the capitalists. In this sense there is no 'managerial revolution' and firms still as ever pursue the highest possible profits. Further, even if managers are assumed to be in control, it is the structure of the capitalist system that will ensure that their behaviour is the same as that of capitalists.

The problem with all of the above approaches is that they are static and ahistorical. They all start from the factual observation of today's dispersed shareholding and attempt to derive conclusions on control by focussing on fixed shareholding percentages possessed by (groups of) shareholders, or by questioning the ability of managers to be independent of all or some shareholders (the neoclassicals and Marxists respectively). Thus they all attempt to infer control today starting from ownership dispersal today.

In this chapter we suggest that a better approach is to start from the beginning, i.e. the undisputed fact of the coexistence of the unity of ownership *and* control in the hands of individual tycoons in the small firms, predecessors of the joint stock companies. We can then analyse the effects of the expansion of firms on the dispersal of corporate ownership and its effects on control. In doing so, we effectively invert the causality underlying the existing approaches, i.e. we attempt to infer control and explain dispersed ownership by starting from the unity of control *and* full ownership. In the light of this approach we suggest that the idea of a 'managerial revolution' is implausible and even inconsistent with its own focus on individual utility maximization. Imposing such an assumption on the original owner-controllers, we suggest, leads smoothly to the conclusion that giant firms today are controlled by a subset of the owners who own a sufficient proportion of aggregate shares to warrant their control of the means of production. This is the Marxist view but with a difference. With dispersed ownership one can only talk about a capitalist class today if one is prepared to accept the proposition that mere partial ownership – albeit sufficient to warrant control over the means of production – is the *sine qua non* of the existence of the definition of such a class. This diverges from the traditional Marxist focus on full ownership and control, but is in line, I think, with the insights of Marxist theory.

A historical overview of the debate[1]

The fatherhood of the 'separation of ownership from control' debate has been attributed to Marx, see, e.g. Aaronovitch (1961), Miliband (1973) and De Vroey (1974). In the third volume of 'Capital' Marx (1959) suggested that the development of the joint stock company tends to separate the management function from the ownership of capital. The non-owner manager, Marx suggested, 'performs the real functions pertaining to the functioning capitalist as such, only the functionary remains and the capitalist disappears as superfluous *from the production process*' (Vol. 3, p. 388, emphasis added). The above does not imply that the capitalist also disappears from society, which becomes obvious when Marx describes what we call here the 'socialization of the ownership of the means of production' (SOMP) as, 'the abolition of capital as private property within the framework of capitalist production itself' (ibid. p. 436).

Perhaps the most important development on this issue along Marxist lines is Hilferding (1981). In his book *Finance Capital*, first published in 1910, Hilferding focussed on the impact of stock dispersion in joint stock companies, on what is in modern usage termed control of 'other peoples' money'. Distinctive about Hilferding's approach is that he viewed the tendency towards SOMP explicitly as a conscious strategy on the part of the controlling capitalists to further their interests by expanding their business. He describes the tendency towards SOMP as a 'distinctive financial technique the aim of which is to ensure control over the largest possible amount of outside capital with the smallest possible amount of one's own capital' (p. 119). As a result, the 'capitalists form an association in the direction of which most have no say.[2] The real control of capital rests with people who have actually contributed only a part of it' (p. 127).

There is no sign of 'managerial revolution' in the sense of management taking control over the means of production, either in Marx or in Hilferding. Both acknowledged the possibility that the separation of the ownership of capital from the unity ownership *and* control might lead to a different attitude on the part of the 'new' type capitalists (partial owners-controllers) compared with that of the 'old' type capitalists (full owners-controllers).[3] This issue was elaborated further by the 'managerialist' school, albeit in a different light.

The idea that the emergence of the joint stock company and the associated tendency towards SOMP will also result in the managerial control of the means of production was forcefully advanced by Berle and Means (1967), in a book first published in 1932. On the theoretical level the Berle and Means' argument was based on the assumption that unless a cohesive group of shareholders owning at least 20% of all shares in a corporation can be identified, this corporation may be assumed to be under management control. On the basis of the above their empirical work suggested that in 1929, 65% of the 200 largest US non-financial corporations were controlled by management.

Based on the Berle and Means' findings, in a book first published in 1942, Burnham (1962) attempted to elevate the idea of management control to a theory of 'social transition [...] from the type of society which we have called capitalist or bourgeois to a type of society which we shall call managerial' (p. 73). Important in Burnham's view was that he saw managers as a 'new class' which controlled not via ownership but via its control of the state mechanism which tended to own the means of production. Burnham suggested that the tendency towards the managerial society was common to capitalist USA, communist USSR and fascist Germany.

Burnham's ideas were discredited soon after their appearance partly because of his unsuccessful prophecies, see e.g. Sweezy (1953). Instead, Berle and Means' position gained widespread acceptance, particularly among industrial economists. The immediate manifestation of that was an outflow of 'managerial' theories of the firm, prominent among which are those of Baumol (1959), Marris (1963, 1967) and Williamson (1964).[4] All these are based on the assumption of managerial control and the associated idea that managers pursue aims (e.g. growth of sales) different from profit maximization, a possibility explicitly acknowledged by Berle and Means and further elaborated by Gordon (1952).[5]

On the empirical level, the neoclassical economists never disputed the 'simple facts [that] only a handful of the largest American corporations can be said to be managed by a coherent group with a major ownership interest. [...] What is in dispute is their implications' (Solow, 1967, p. 103). Regarding in particular the aims of the giant corporations, the capital market discipline will ensure that managers will never significantly diverge from the profit maximization aim. If they do, the stock market will put a low valuation to the firm's assets that will tempt another management to take over the non-profit-maximizing firm; this obviously constitutes 'a definite threat to the management taken over' (ibid. p. 107).

Similar considerations moreover apply to other types of corporate decisions, e.g. the decisions over what to pay out to the shareholders in the form of dividends. If shareholders do not like their management's policies they can always sell their shares. It follows that the shareholders as a body *are* in effective control of the firms they 'own'. The move from owner-managed to management-managed firms does not imply loss of owner's control to managers but simply the sharing of control more or less equally between all the shareholders, who as a group are still interested in maximum profits.

The idea that managerialism leads to no qualitative differences as regards the functioning of the capitalist system is advocated by some Marxist economists. Baran and Sweezy (1967), for example, accepted the idea that today's giant firms are controlled from within by their professional managers. Still, the very class structure of the capitalist system, they argued, ensures that managers are recruited from the highest cosietal echelons, the wealthiest of the wealthy, and share the aims and aspirations (or they are themselves members) of the capitalist class. In this sense capitalists are still in control of the giant firms. It is only the small-level shareholders who are divorced from effective control. The controlling managers are still only interested in maximizing profits, the source of funds for expansion and growth. That profit maximization is still the aim of the firms, even if managerialism is accepted, is also reinforced by the possibility that profits may be a necessary prerequisite for the achievement of other 'managerial' objectives, see Cowling (1982).

Despite the preoccupation of a significant number of neoclassical and Marxist economists with the implications of the 'managerial revolution' rather than its existence, a number of economists mainly in the latter tradition also questioned the very idea that managers do control. Important contributions along these lines are, e.g. Mills (1959), Aaronovitch (1961) and Miliband (1973). Essentially, this approach consists of trying to identify empirically the existence of a 'power elite' 'ruling class' and/or 'capitalist class', which owns and controls the means of production, and then show that managers are either recruited from the capitalist class or are assimilated by it.

The above criticisms of the proponents of the 'managerial revolution' and in particular the extensive empirical evidence marshalled mainly by Marxist economists, are indicative of the severe limitations of the managerialist arguments. However, they do not constitute a fundamental theoretical attack on the latter because they do not question the basic managerialist framework; they attempt statically to identify a capitalist class today and thus deduce control today, rather than attempting to examine dynamically what happens over time to control by analysing the potential impact of firms' expansion on corporate ownership. The basic tenets of such an approach, which follows Hilferding (1981) and Pitelis and Sugden (1986), are outlined below.

The meaning of control, expansion, finance and management

Throughout this chapter we follow Zeitlin (1974) in defining control as the ability to determine broad corporate objectives despite resistance from others. The expression 'broad corporate objectives' refers to decisions taken over strategic issues such as the firms' relationship with rivals, the geographical orientation of the firm, its relationship with the state, foreign governments, workers, sources of raw materials, etc. Control in this sense does not refer to day-to-day operational decisions on tactical issues, e.g. promotional activities, etc. The latter, albeit important for the short-run smooth functioning of the firm, are by their very nature of lesser importance than the strategic decisions as regards the long-run success or failure of the firm – simply because they are subject to the constraints imposed on them by the strategic decisions. Similar considerations apply to working decisions, i.e. those taken by workers as regards, e.g. work intensity, etc., and which are subject to the constraints of both the strategic and operational decisions.

Those in control need not necessarily be those who implement strategic decisions. The latter task may be left with others specifically employed to do that. These individuals may also be given discretion as regards the best way of implementing a decision. If those implementing the decisions attempt to replace a strategic decision with another not favoured by the original decision makers, and they succeed, we have a *transfer of control*. If they fail, and as a result are perhaps punished for their behaviour (sacked or not promoted), control remains with the original decision makers. This will be defined as *actual* control. In practice the implementation of the original decision will tend to be ensured by the very possibility that the transfer of control may not be easy and that the potential consequences of failure may be punishment. In this case control is *potential*, i.e. not associated with specific actions by the original decision makers. Still, it is equally real, see Zeitlin (1974), Nyman and Silberston (1978).

Consider now a small pre-joint-stock-company firm, owned, managed and controlled by its owners, 'capitalists'. Workers in the firm are employed to perform designated tasks and take working decisions. Strategic and operational decisions are with the capitalists. Assuming that at a certain stage of its development such a firm decides to expand, we address ourselves to the question whether 'capitalist(s)' lose their control of the firm.

Assuming first that the capitalists are rational individuals in the neoclassical and managerialist sense of utility maximization, i.e. not satiated in the consumption of any two goods (here control and expansion), it follows immediately that in deciding to expand capitalists are also willing to retain control. It may even be that the controlling capitalists of the small firm expand the latter because they are willing to be in control of a larger firm. Under our assumption, capitalists will only lose control of the expanded firm if they voluntarily decide to do this, or if they cannot expand *and* retain control.

This last possibility is the concern of the managerialists, see e.g. the discussion in Marris and Mueller (1980). Expansion requires finance. To the extent that the original capitalists' fortunes are sufficient to warrant the necessary expansion, the latter does not pose any problems as regards control. If, however, capitalists' own finance is insufficient they will have to obtain more, either from other capitalists, industrial or financial, or from the public, by issuing shares and selling them to those willing and able to buy them. Both the above possibilities entail a potential loss of control. In the former case loss of control may be the effective price of borrowing, supposing e.g. the capitalists fail to pay back the loans. Another possibility is that capitalists will have to share their control with their borrowers. Although at the aggregate level this possibility does not pose problems to the manager *versus* capitalist control issue since control is still with capitalists, for the individual rational capitalist the price is very high and the situation one to be avoided. In this sense going public may be a better alternative.[6]

The decision to issue shares to the public is capitalists' own decision as it is the extent to which new shares will be issued. The rational capitalists will (can) sell shares (i.e. divorce themselves from part of the firm's ownership) up to their subjectively perceived maximum point where further sale of shares will imply loss of their control, i.e. loss of their ability to take the strategic decisions and be confident that they will be able to see them implemented. It is only if the critical share ownership percentage required to ensure control on their part is exceeded that capitalists will lose control. Under our rationality assumption capitalists will never *voluntarily* exceed this critical point. Given that the sale of shares is their own decision, it follows that one should generally not expect expansion to be associated with loss of control, unless capitalists have miscalculated the critical percentage required for maintenance of control.

The latter possibility cannot be excluded on *a priori* grounds. In the limiting case all capitalists in all firms can miscalculate this critical percentage. The capitalists may then be obliged to share control with other capitalists who have bought a proportion of the firm's shares sufficient to ensure control of the firm if added to that of the original controllers. Alternatively the original controllers may totally lose control to another group of capitalists owning sufficient shares to allow them to exercise unfettered control. Finally control may be lost to other groups, e.g. managers or even workers.

The first two eventualities appear possible but do not pose problems to the capitalists *versus* managers control issue since in the aggregate capitalists remain in control. It should be noted, however, that the possibility of total displacement of the original capitalists by others is not easy as it is plausible to expect that the original capitalists, being insiders, will in general need a lower percentage of shares than an external group in order to exercise control, a proposition well in line with the existing empirical evidence, see e.g. Herman (1979).[7]

The possibility that control will be lost to managers, our focus here, is therefore just one of many. Expansion involves both the need for finance, and the appearance of a managerial group. The larger and more complex a firm becomes, the more difficult it becomes for the original capitalists to administer it on their own. A group of people specially trained to do so is required. Similarly a group of technical experts and scientists is required for research and development.[8] This managerial group, or technostructure, inevitably acquires internal knowledge of the firm's operations. It might therefore appear tempting to suggest *ex-post* that, in the absence of a capitalist group sufficiently informed on the internal operations of the firm, management might be able to have effective control as a result of their access to and manipulation of their internal knowledge.

From an *ex-ante* point of view, this is not plausible. As in the case of the selling of shares, the appointment of a manager or technical expert is originally the decision of the controlling capitalists. It follows that it is up to them to appoint a person from their immediate milieu or, at all events, someone who appears to share their aspirations and world outlook. This does not preclude the possibility that the 'wrong' person might be appointed and/or that gradually managers might develop interests of their own and try to pursue them even at the expense of the capitalists, e.g. by distorting information they pass to the capitalists. However, it is very unlikely that such a situation will ever reach a stage when a strategic decision is effectively set aside and a new one implemented without the controlling capitalists realizing what is going on and perhaps as a result sacking the managers.[9] Simply because the original controllers can always see to it that one of themselves is top manager within the firm they can ensure access to the necessary information as to whether a strategic decision is being implemented.[10] This possibility is intuitively appealing since it would be surprising if, historically, the expansion of firms coincided with *all* capitalists deciding at the same time to withdraw from management. Some will and some will not – because managing *per se* gives them satisfaction or because they think it ensures the 'proper' operation of the firm (e.g. it pre-empts a prospective managerial threat), or both.[11]

The above suggestions are well in line with the existing extensive evidence, e.g. in Nichols (1969), Miliband (1973) and Francis (1980a), that, in general, managers do share the same social background, education, outlook and aspirations as the big shareholders. In our framework this empirical finding is an implication of the analysis, rather than *ex-post* support to the capitalist control idea.

To summarize, under the assumption that capitalists are rational, one should expect them both to retain, following expansion, a sufficient part of shares to ensure their control, and to have access to sufficient information to ensure their ability to take the strategic decisions and see them implemented. The managerialist view is thus implausible even in its own framework. It can only be sustained under the assumptions that *all* shareholders in *all* firms misjudge the critical percentage required for them to exercise control, and/or fail to ensure access to internal information about the firm and that, given the above, no other group of capitalists has stepped in to share control with the original capitalists, or to totally displace them.

The analysis has so far been based on the assumption that capitalists are rational in the sense of non-satiation in expansion and control. In practice capitalists may not be willing to have either or both. For example, they may not want to expand partly because expansion entails a potential loss or sharing of control, which they may not view as desirable. Hannah (1976) has ample historical evidence for the UK suggesting that in the early nineteenth century a widespread preference for small family-controlled enterprises constituted an important brake on external growth through mergers. One could suggest that this preference might also apply in the case of internal expansion and thus brake it. On the other hand, individual capitalists may decide to relinquish control, e.g. for reasons associated with their age, preference for more leisure, etc. In this case one should expect control to pass to their heirs, or, in the latter's absence and/or unwillingness to take over, to other capitalists, managers and even workers. In this case, however, the latter gain control by themselves becoming capitalists, i.e. by fully owning and controlling the firm, or by owning sufficient shares to ensure their control. Similar considerations moreover apply in the case of a capitalist's death.[12]

More generally the possibility that managers and/or workers will be upwardly mobile, i.e. gain control by becoming capitalists themselves, need not be confined to the unlikely contingency of their becoming the original capitalists' heirs. Although such mobility is certainly not widespread in capitalist countries, see Miliband (1973) for evidence, it is certainly not impossible, particularly in the case of managers, see Gerth and Mills (1952). It is theoretically plausible and well in line with the existing evidence, see e.g. Sawyer (1979), that top managers, even if they begin their careers with no ownership stakes in the firm, receive shares as part of their payment, and/or buy themselves shares in the firms they manage. In so doing managers become capitalists themselves and in this sense top managers may exercise control of some firms. This, however, is capitalist control. It is simply the case that top managers join the ranks of the capitalist class.[13] The essence of the argument lies in its stress on the importance of shareownership for the exercise of control. The analysis obviously accommodates the idea that managers or workers can obtain control by acquiring sufficient shares, while, on the other hand, failed capitalists may become managers or workers, see e.g. Marx (1959). For the purposes of the capitalists *versus* managers control debate, the essence is capitalist control.

The importance of share-ownership for the exercise of control lies in the fact that in the joint stock company strategic decisions can be voted upon and therefore determined at shareholders' meetings. The ability to win such votes may therefore determine who controls the firm; possession of sufficient votes will imply control. 'Sufficient' in the above sense may be as little as 2% or 1% of shares, see Cubbin and Leech (1983), depending on the dispersal of shareholding, whether control is exercised internally or externally, and the degree of collusion between groupings of both big-level and small-level shareholders.

The issue, in particular, of the possibility of small shareholders colluding raises the important question as to whether the neoclassical hypothesis that shareholders as a body are in control of firms (rather than my hypothesis) is true. If all the small-level shareholders can act as a group, or alternatively react to undesired decisions by selling their shares, they may be argued to be effectively in control of the firm. The latter possibility is examined in detail in the next chapter. The idea that all shareholders will be able to collude seems implausible. Most small-level shareholders do not buy shares with an eye to control, but rather in order to receive dividends and perhaps capital gains, see Scott (1985). They have little or no access to independent information, and thus are easily manipulated by the big shareholders and high-level managers with big ownership stakes.[14] The neoclassical hypothesis is thus implausible, both under its own assumptions of individual utility maximization but also for all the reasons that the managerialists have advanced to dispute owner control, i.e. wide dispersal of ownership and limited access to internal information of the firm's activities.

In our framework the managerialist view may then be seen as an effective attack on the neoclassical view within the latter's own framework. Both views, however, share the idea that no subset of the shareholders exists which, by virtue of ownership, can control both the managers and the small-level shareholders. Both views are thus inconsistent with their own focus on individual utility maximization, if the latter is applied to the original owners-controllers. The tendency towards SOMP has not resulted in a separation of ownership from control but rather in a separation of *part* of ownership from the unity full ownership *and* control.

The above conclusion is in line with the Marxist view on the issue, but with a difference. Our conclusion was obtained by inverting the causal direction implicit in the arguments of all managerialist, neoclassical and Marxist theorists, who attempted to infer control statically by observing today's dispersed shareholding. Instead, we examined simultaneously the results of expanding firms on the dispersal of shareownership and control.

Also consistent with the Marxist view is the implication of our analysis that since capitalists are still in control of firms, one should reasonably expect their aims to be the same, that is, to strive for the highest possible profits. In fact the separation of ownership from management may be facilitating the achievement of this aim. Firstly because of the technical expertise and training of the managers, see Baran and Sweezy (1967); secondly, because, as Hilferding (1981) has observed, the interests of the non-controlling shareholders may be acting as a constraint on the capitalist greed for profits, and as a result may increase rationalization within the firm and thus possibly the long-run profits.[15]

Perhaps more significant is that in our framework the tendency towards the socialization of the ownership of the means of production and the associated idea of a 'managerialist revolution' can be seen as the result of the strive for profits (i.e. expansion for increased accumulation of capital), rather than the reason for this strive ceasing to be the motive of giant enterprises, the managerialist view.

Some existing evidence

A substantial number of studies have attempted to test empirically the above alternative hypotheses, either directly or indirectly by focussing on the potentially different implications of the rival views.

In the orthodox economics literature attempts to distinguish between different theories are basically of the indirect type. They are mainly concerned with the issues of profit versus growth of sales maximization, the 'unprofitability' of mergers and the observed 'excessive' retention ratios, i.e. pay-out ratios lower than those favoured by small-level shareholders. It is alleged in particular that 'unprofitable' mergers and 'excessive' retention ratios are not compatible with the neoclassical view and therefore that they imply the managerialist view is correct.

The problem with empirical studies on profit *versus* growth of sales maximization is that, first, they rely on the assumption that it is possible to use the managerialist approach, i.e. to focus on *ad hoc* shareholding percentages, in order to classify firms as either manager or owner controlled. In this sense, these studies assume what is under question. In addition, they assume that, granted our ability to distinguish between manager- and owner-controlled firms, the two will differ in the aims they pursue. Given the above, it is no surprise that the result of such studies was inconclusive, see Herman (1979) for a survey, and Sawyer (1979). Similar considerations apply for the finding of the so-called 'unprofitable' mergers, see Aaronovitch and Sawyer (1975). Further, 'excessive' retention ratios are at least as compatible with capitalist control as they are with managerialist control, see Kalecki (1971). In this sense, as it will be detailed in the next chapter, the issue of 'excessive' retention ratios casts severe theoretical and empirical doubt only on the neoclassical hypothesis that shareholders as a body are in control of firms.

Three phenomena which have recently aroused increasing interest provide indirect evidence against the managerialist view; the growth of shareownership by financial institutions, the emergence of the M-form organization, and the appearance of management buy-outs.

In all major capitalist countries, the tendency towards dispersal of shareownership was soon followed by a counter-tendency towards concentration of control over shareownership in the hands of a few financial institutions, in particular merchant banks, pension funds and insurance companies, see Scott (1985) for evidence. In the UK, for example, aggregate personal share-ownership declined from around 66% in 1957 to around 23% in 1985. In the same period the share-ownership by financial institutions increased from 21.3% to just over 60%. This tendency towards concentration of share-ownership is in direct contrast to the managerialist tenet that managers control because share-ownership is widely dispersed. Difficult as it is to maintain that managers control because no big shareholders exist, the task becomes impossible in the face of highly concentrated shareholdings in the hands of financial capitalists.

By virtue of their ownership stakes in firms, financial institutions will be expected to display a keen interest in the performance of the industrial corporations, especially if it is accepted that it is on the latter's profits that the very existence of the financial companies depends, see e.g. Hilferding (1981).[16] To the extent that such stakes are large enough to ensure control on their part, or to oblige industrial capitalists to share control with them, share-ownership by the financial institutions may be indicative of a tendency towards corporate control by finance (industrial and financial) capital, rather than managerial control.

Also of interest is the emergence of the M-form organization, i.e. the transition of many firms in the US, the UK and Europe from the so-called U-form to the M-form organization. The U-form organization was characterized by a board of directors and various divisions, each responsible for a specific function, e.g. production, marketing, etc., throughout the firm. Williamson (1970) suggested that as a U-form firm expands, there is a tendency for strategic and operational decisions to become entangled. In contrast the M-form organization is characterized by a board of directors responsible solely for determining strategic decisions, and a series of operating divisions, each responsible for its own operational decisions. The importance of the M-form, as Herman (1979) observed, is that, by reducing interdependence and establishing each division as a profit centre, it enlarges the possibilities for centralized evaluation and control; thus is restricts managerial control to its proper sphere, operational decisions.

The irony of the almost simultaneous appearance of the idea of a 'managerialist revolution' in the 1930s and the rapid spread of divisionalization with its effects on restoring goal specification and policing processes led Williamson himself to reconsider his views on the separation of ownership from control. By activating the market for corporate control, Williamson (1981) suggests, management was brought under the scrutiny of the general office, which 'can be regarded as the agent of the stockholders, whose purpose is to monitor the operations of the constituent parts' (p. 1559).

In the light of all this Williamson attributes the Berle and Means findings to the then prevalence of the U-form, and concludes that the dilemma regarding corporate control posed by Berle and Means has since been alleviated more by internal organizational reforms than by regulatory or external ones.

Williamson's view that the idea of a 'managerial revolution' is not compatible with the transition towards the M-form organization is certainly a sound one. Where we differ is over his view of the general office as the 'agent' of all the stockholders. In our framework one should expect the general office to be the 'agent' of a subset of the stockholders, capitalists. The tendency towards concentration of share-ownership in the hands of the financiers and the empirical evidence that the ultimate beneficiaries of these shares – e.g. workers in the case of pension funds, have no control over these shares, see Minns (1981) – is certainly in line with this view. In our framework the transition to the M-form can be seen partly as an attempt on the part of the controlling capitalists to pre-empt a situation of continuously increasing 'control loss', see Williamson (1967), arising out of the multiplicity of decision layers in the large corporations, resulting in 'loss of control' to the operational decision makers, managers, due to lack of information on the part of capitalists or managers.[17] Similar to our arguments regarding (access to) internal information, internal reorganizations by the controlling capitalists are seen here as a means of ensuring that their control is not lost. This view is more moderate than that of Williamson's whose original acceptance of the Berle and Means findings would lead us to believe that the M-form can be seen as a counter-revolution of the stockholders to the 'managerialist revolution'.

Also of interest in our discussion is the management buy-out phenomenon. In recent years an increasing number of corporate managers in the US and the UK have bought the companies or parts of the companies they managed, following the retirement of the controlling capitalists (particularly in the case of smaller firms) and in the absence or unwillingness of heirs to take the latter over, or as a defence to a threat of acquisition, see Wright and Coyne (1985). The finance for the management buy-out is normally provided by financial institutions which in their turn may put their representatives on the board of the firm. As a result, control of the firm after the buy-out is with the new owner-managers and/or the financial institutions which provided the finance.

The management buy-out phenomenon further confirms my emphasis on the importance of share-ownership in the exercise of control and my suggestion that managers can only become controllers by becoming capitalists. This is exactly what the owners–managers attempt to do following a buy-out. Whether they succeed depends partly upon their ability to repay the borrowed funds. In any case, however, it is owner-managers and/or financial institutions which end up in control of the firms. The end product of management buy-outs is more firms being controlled through a shareholding sufficient to ensure such control.

It is reasonable, I think, to conclude, on the basis of the above, that all the existing indirect evidence either does not support, or indeed contradicts the idea of a 'managerial revolution'. It appears to be well in line with my proposition that capitalists control the giant corporations.

Similar conclusions may be drawn from the existing direct evidence. This evidence can be classified into three basic categories. The first criticizes managerialists' reliance on *fixed ad-hoc* shareholding percentages because this ignores that the higher is the degree of dispersal of share-ownership, the lower is the shareholding percentage needed for control to be exercised by an individual or few holdings, see e.g. Cubbin and Leech (1983). Evidence along these lines by Leech (1984) involved formalizing the Berle and Means assumptions in a probabilistic voting model, and reinterpreting their data taking into account shareholding dispersal. Assuming collusive behaviour on the part of the top 20 shareholders, an assumption well in line with Berle and Means' definition of minority control, Leech assigned 11 out of the 16 Berle and Means' management-controlled firms to the minority-controlled category.

A second type of direct evidence has been obtained by either accepting the managerialist *ad-hoc* fixed-percentage criterion, or rejecting it for a 'more plausible' (still fixed and *ad-hoc*) lower one and then proceeding to show that this percentage is more often held by a group of owners than the managerialists would have us believe. This is achieved by attempting to identify kinship networks, interlocking directorates, secrecy-based methods of control and other such 'hidden' ways by which a group of capitalists may exercise control, see Scott and Hughes (1976). An example along these lines is provided by the latter authors. They analysed 220 Scottish registered firms with stock exchange quotations and initially concluded that in 77% of cases an individual institution or cohesive group owned at least 5% of the shares. These were classified as owner-controlled firms. They then examined in more detail the residual 23% and found that even among the latter more detailed analysis could identify more owner-controlled firms.

The above study is representative of this type of analysis but by no means unique. In fact the evidence along these lines is huge and well beyond the scope of this chapter to survey. Such a detailed survey is given in Scott (1985). Suffice it to note here that all such evidence suggests strongly that emphasis on the presumed managerial dominance is misplaced, to say the least.

The types of direct evidence cited here are very important in that they question managerialism within the latter's own methodological framework, i.e. assuming or estimating a shareholding percentage necessary for control and then trying to identify whether a group of owners holds it. Such evidence becomes even more damaging to the managerialist position if taken together. That is, if the Scott and Hughes' type of approach were used after the shareholding percentage had been estimated, as in e.g. the study by Leech, it is plausible to suggest that more owner-controlled firms might have been identified, depending on the degree of shareholding dispersion.

A third type of direct evidence departs from the managerialist focus on shareholding percentages. It attempts to examine the policies actually pursued by firms, and tries to assess whether or not they appear to be determined by owners or managers. Interesting examples along these lines are Nyman and Silberston (1978) and Francis (1980). The latter author, for example, suggested that the vital role within a firm is played by the chairperson at the board; this is apparently a clear result of the Oxford Growth of Firms project upon which the analysis was based. On this basis, Francis suggested that a detailed examination of the identity of the chairperson (whether e.g. an owner or a professional manager), or the history of the chairperson's appointment (e.g. by owners or managers) might reveal the centre of control in the firm.

Francis examined in detail 17 firms randomly drawn from a sample of 227 of the 'top 250' UK companies in the 'Times 1000' (1975–76). From these 227, in 110 at least 5% of shares was found to be held by owners. From the 17 firms analysed in detail along the lines suggested above, 15 were classified as owner-controlled and only two controlled by their professional managers.

There is no doubt that none of the above evidence is conclusive. In Francis' case, for example, the sample analysed in detail is very small. One could also question the importance of the 'chairperson of the board' criterion. Granted these reservations, however, it seems to me reasonable to conclude on the basis of the above that all the existing direct evidence on the separation of ownership and control issue cast doubt on the idea of a 'managerial revolution'. The more one relaxes the assumptions underlying the Berle and Means' methodology, the more owner-controlled firms one tends to identify. In this sense the direct evidence examined here offers support to the theoretical analysis of control in this chapter as did the indirect evidence discussed earlier.

It is worth emphasizing that the inversion of the causality of the managerialist methodology pursued in this chapter led to the conclusion that in a capitalist society capitalists will always be in control of firms, either because capitalists will never forfeit control, or because, if they do, control will pass to other capitalists, i.e. groups of individuals (including ex-managers and/or ex-workers) or institutions who control the firms by holding sufficient shares to ensure their control. The few firms classified as manager-controlled in the studies examined above would most probably in a still-more-detailed examination be revealed as capitalist-controlled.

In conclusion, I advanced above the proposition that a subset of the owners should still be expected to control the giant firms by virtue of their share-ownership in these firms, and defined this group as capitalists. Indeed one could use alternatives such as a 'ruling class', see Aaronovitch (1961), a 'capitalist class', see Miliband (1973), or a 'constellation of interests', see

Scott (1985). Any of these titles will do to describe the essence of our point here, that giant firms are controlled by a subset of their owners, and through partial ownership. The importance of the tendency towards the SOMP is thus not to be found in capitalists losing control to managers. Rather it is to be found in the former's ability to control the firms through merely partial ownership and, as a result, also to control the funds of the vast majority of shareholders who collectively 'own' the firm. It is this control over other people's money that raises very important questions both at the microeconomic level of individual choice, and the macroeconomic performance of capitalist economics as a whole. These issues are addressed in the rest of this book.

CHAPTER 3

Shareownership and 'social' choice

At the microeconomic or individual level the tendency towards the socialization of the ownership of the means of production (SOMP) and its associated possibility that not all shareholders are in control of firms raises the important question as to whether corporate policies represent a consensus outcome of all shareholders' preferences, or rather an imposition of the preferences of some controlling shareholders and/or managers on the rest, the non-controlling shareholders. Particularly important is the decision as to what proportion of profits to pay out as dividends to the shareholders, the pay-out ratio, which simultaneously determines the part of profit retained within the corporation, the retention ratio. The importance of this decision arises from the possibility that changes in the retention ratio may lead to changes in the proportion of private (personal plus corporate) income saved for the purpose of capital accumulation. In addition, given that, unless such changes are in line with the preferences of all shareholders, the location of control within the giant corporation may be directly linked with financial capital accumulation, through constraining the choices of the non-controlling shareholders as to what proportion of their private disposable income they will consume/save. This latter possibility has become the subject of debate between three different schools of thought in economics; the neoclassicals, the managerialists and the Marxists.

In the neoclassical tradition the possibility that corporate decisions on retentions may not reflect the preferences of all shareholders does not arise. The ultimate power of the shareholders lies with their ability to sell their shares. This obliges the managers of the firms to take decisions in line with the preferences of all shareholders. Alternatively, if shareholders observe that the retention ratio is not in line with their preferences, they can simply offset its effects on capital accumulation by changing the part of their personal disposable income they save in the opposite direction. In both the above cases, the outcome is a 'consensus' one, i.e. the private saving to income ratio reflects all shareholders' preferences.

In stark contrast to the above view, the proponents of the 'managerial revolution' idea suggested that corporate policies on retentions act as a constraint on the consumption/saving decisions of *all* shareholders. Under the assumption that non-shareholder managers control the firms and maximize a different utility function to that of the shareholders, managerialists suggest that managers will favour high retentions while shareholders will go for high dividends. Given their control, managers will impose their 'preferences' on the shareholders who will not be fully able to offset managers' policies. This induces a positive link between managerial control and financial capital accumulation, by restricting shareholders' consumption.

The importance of corporate retentions has also been acknowledged in the Marxist tradition, although few attempts have been made seriously to examine their impact on individual choice. The most notable exception broadly in this tradition is Marglin (1975). He mounted a severe attack on neoclassical ideas by endorsing the managerial views on control and preference for retentions and by pointing to the preoccupation of shareholders with consuming all their disposable income, as well as the constraints they face in borrowing. The end product of all this, he suggested, would be a one-to-one correspondence between managers' decisions on retentions and financial capital accumulation.

The asymmetry in choice highlighted by the managerial position need not be grounded on a distinction between (controlling) managers, on the one hand, and (non-controlling) body of shareholders on the other. It can equally be seen in terms of a distinction between controlling shareholder-capitalists, on the one hand, and non-controlling shareholders on the other.

As indicated in the previous chapter, this distinction is preferable to the managerialist both in terms of theory and the existing evidence. It also allows new insights to be gained into this important issue. In particular, we suggest in this chapter, that by adopting the above distinction we can conclude that the neoclassical proposition is correct for the case of controlling shareholders, but incorrect for the case of non-controlling shareholders, for whom the managerialist analysis is closer to reality. Corporate decisions on retained earnings do not constrain the choices of those who take the decisions, the controlling capitalists, but they do constrain the choices of the non-controlling shareholders. Changes in the retention ratio will thus positively affect financial capital accumulation, the aggregate effect being a function of the proportion of shares owned by the controlling group, as well as the extent to which non-controlling shareholders are constrained in their attempts to react to undesired corporate decisions. That the latter may be severely constrained is ensured by the fact (among others) that the vast majority of non-controlling shareholders today do not own shares directly but rather indirectly through their participation in an occupational pension fund scheme. The transition from direct (discretionary) share-ownership to indirect (compulsory) shareownership which arose through the so-called pension funds revolution, mainly in the US and the UK, has been disregarded by both the neoclassicists and their critics. Its importance lies in that it removes from the non-controlling shareholders their ultimate weapon, of selling their shares, as the actual control of their shareholding does not lie with the participants in the pension fund scheme – normally workers – but rather the firms or financial institutions which manage the funds.

It follows that the emergence of indirect shareownership through pension funds ensures that the vast majority of non-controlling shareholders will be unable to react to corporate retained earnings decisions by selling their shares. Furthermore, the pension funds revolution introduces another source of corporate saving and a route through which 'social' choice may be further constrained, i.e. the part of the pension funds' income arising from total contributions, not paid back to workers as benefits – the net inflow into pension funds – is not disposable to the participants. To the extent that participants in the schemes are unaware of the full amount of their pension funds rights and/or constrained in attempting to affect increases in the net inflow to pension funds, such increases will also have a positive impact on financial capital accumulation, again arising from restrictions on social choice.

Direct shareownership and 'social' choice

The potential link between direct share-ownership, the voluntary buying of shares by individuals, and the choice of these individuals as to what part of their income to consume/save and therefore aggregate financial capital accumulation, has attracted the interest of the neoclassical theorists as well as their managerialist and Marxist critics.[1]

In the neoclassical tradition two basic variations may be identified. For Solow (1967), for example, the ability of shareholders to sell their shares by simply 'telephoning their brokers' implies that shareholders as a body are in control of firms. The selling of shares will tend to drive share prices down, thus attracting a potential take-over, with its associated risk of the managers of the firms being replaced. This capital market discipline therefore will ensure that those in the day-to-day management of the firms will take decisions in line with the interests of all shareholders. Corporate decisions on retained earnings do not constrain the implementation of the consumption/saving decisions of the shareholders, simply because the latter are in effective control of the firms.

For Modigliani (1970), the possibility that corporate decisions on retained earnings may not be taken in such a way as to reflect all shareholders' wishes is allowed. In this case, however, it is argued that inter-temporal utility-maximizing individuals will realize that, as a result of changes in corporate retained earnings, their total (corporate plus personal) saving may exceed the level they would have chosen if in control of firms, and therefore they will try to offset, e.g. corporate retention increases by reducing their personal saving. Provided that shareholders are fully able to both 'pierce the corporate veil', Feldstein (1973), and reduce their personal saving sufficiently, corporate retentions and personal saving can be regarded as perfect substitutes. In this sense shareholders defy any attempts by firms' controllers to restrict their choice over their consumption/saving plans, and ensure that the private (corporate plus personal) saving ratio, i.e. private sector financial capital accumulation, is in line with all shareholders' preferences.

It follows that both Solow's and Modigliani's versions consistently reject the possibility that at least some shareholders' choices will be constrained by corporate decisions on retentions. This harmony view was challenged within the neoclassical tradition by Harrod (1948), to whom surprisingly Modigliani (1975) has attributed the fatherhood of the perfect substitutability of saving thesis. Indeed, although Harrod did consider it plausible that individual shareholders may regard corporate retentions as theirs, and thus a substitute for their personal saving, he also suggested that it was 'conceivable that corporate saving might exceed the total that all individuals would be disposed to save ...' (p. 48). Thus increases in corporate saving may increase private saving through restricting the choices of some shareholders, implying an imperfect substitution between corporate and personal saving.

Harrod gave no justification for his suggestion that imperfect substitution is possible. The predominant neoclassical position today is that of perfect substitution, see e.g. Feldstein (1973), Dixit (1976), namely that households will fully offset undesired changes in corporate retentions by adjusting their consumption/saving behaviour. Harrod's idea has been revived by the proponents of the managerial revolution thesis, albeit in a different framework.

The managerialist position is based on the assumption that managers control the firms and maximize a utility function different than that of the shareholders. It is then suggested that managers exhibit a stronger preference for retentions than shareholders do. The main reasons for this posited asymmetry in the preferences of all shareholders on the one hand and managers on the other are the 'consuming nature' of our society and the risks associated with external borrowing.

For corporate retentions to increase, shareholders should abstain from current consumption. This is not desirable on their part as the advertising and other selling activities of the corporate sector will tend to induce shareholders to consume as much income as they can get. Thus shareholders will favour a low retention ratio, or at least one that is not increasing over time. As managers are assumed not to own shares, they are not required to consume less when there is an increase in the retention ratio. In fact they will tend to favour high retention ratios, preferably increasing over time, mainly due to their preference for growth through retained profits, itself induced from the risks associated with external borrowing, see e.g. Marris (1967), Galbraith (1967). As the latter author puts it:

> Control of the supply of savings is strategic for industrial planning [. . .] apart from the normal disadvantages of an uncertain price, there is a danger that under some circumstances supply will not be forthcoming at an acceptable price. This will be at the precise moment when misfortune or miscalculation has made the need more urgent [. . .] Money carries with it the special right to know and even to suggest, how it is used. This dilutes the authority of the planning unit (pp. 55–6).

It follows that non-owner managers prefer a higher retention ratio to that favoured by shareholders. As they are assumed to control the firm, they impose their preferences on the shareholders, and corporate retentions increase. Provided that there is no perfect substitutability between corporate retentions and personal saving, managerial decisions increase private saving–financial capital accumulation.

Marris (1967) considered it plausible that such substitutability might be less than perfect. In its simplest form Marris' argument is as follows. Suppose all profits were distributed to the shareholders as dividends. Some shareholders would, as a result, definitely increase their consumption while others might keep it constant. It follows that the very existence of share-ownership and retained earnings implies that consumption is reduced by the exact amount by which some shareholders would, in the absence of retentions, have increased their consumption. Thus, increases in retentions will also result in increasing private saving. For the latter to be constant under the above assumptions, some shareholders would have to reduce their consumption following an increase in their dividends-disposable income; this Marris finds implausible. Thus he concludes that 'under the actual circumstances of both today and yesterday, long run variations in the retention ratio must cause long run variations in the national propensity to save (in the same direction, of course, but smaller in magnitude), even when distributive shares are held constant' (p. 295).

Other factors that may reinforce managers' preference for a high retention ratio are a presumed positive link between high retentions and the growth rate of managerial bonuses, see Marris (1967, p. 69), as well as tax advantages associated with retained profits, see Hay and Morris (1979). The latter may obviously induce a high preference for retentions in shareholders as well. Still it is very unlikely that the preferences of managers and the shareholders will coincide, due to the positive impact of advertising and other selling/promotion activities on the part of the firms on the shareholders' preference for consumption. In stark contrast to the neoclassical idea of consumer sovereignty where advertising has little – if any – role to play, see e.g. Green (1971), for the managerialists the preferences of the consumers are effectively controlled by Madison Avenue, i.e. are too malleable to be relied upon when it comes to such an important issue as capital accumulation. This malleability and its associated preference for shareholders' current consumptions outweighs any positive impact that tax advantages may have on shareholders' preferences for retentions. This necessitates the removal of the capital accumulation function from the shareholders to the non-shareholding managers. As Galbraith (1967) puts it:

it would be highly inconsistent for a society which so values consumption, and so relentlessly presses its claims, to rely on consumers, through their savings, for its capital [. . .] In a society which so emphasises consumption and so needs capital the decision to save should obviously be removed from the consumer and exercised by other authority (ibid. p. 55).

For modern capitalist societies this is done 'in the main by the management of a few hundred corporations' (ibid. p. 57).

It can be concluded from the above that according to the managerialist position it is the (assumption of a) managerialist revolution that ensures the continuation of the capital accumulation process in advanced capitalist societies. In its absence this process might have come to a virtual standstill; for there are simply no groups of shareholders – capitalists – who might be prepared to undertake this function. This view is also shared by neoclassicists, a fact that partly clouds the apparent differences between the two theories.

In the broad Marxist tradition Marglin (1975, 1975a) mounted a powerful attack on the neoclassical idea of perfect substitution, both in theory and by showing econometrically that his rather 'simple' 'growth of incomes' model of the consumption function can perform at least equally as well as the most elaborate of the 'orthodox' models – Friedman's (1957) Permanent Income Hypothesis and the Life Cycle Hypothesis of Ando and Modigliani (1963).[2] In doing so, however, and despite his explicit recognition of the existence of classes and class interests, Marglin adopts an essentially managerialist standpoint.

Starting from the managerialist position that corporate control is with managers, Marglin (1975) suggests that:

the rate of capital formation remains reasonably high in capitalist societies because hierarchical organisation permits a relatively small number of individuals to decide how much the rest of us will save. If, by contrast, savings decisions were left to individuals – whether capitalists or workers – accumulation of productive capital [. . .] would come to a virtual standstill (1975, p. 20).

Modern corporate management obliges workers as well as nominal owners of capital to provide for their collective future [. . .] (ibid. p. 22).

He thus appears to be in line with the managerialist ideas on this issue.

Regarding the managerialists' presumption that controlling managers exhibit a strong preference for internal finance through retained earnings, in order to maximize their own utility functions, Marglin suggests that: 'It is undoubtedly more realistic to interpret corporate savings decisions in terms of managers' perceptions of their own interest: managerial power, prestige, and income are all furthered by plowing back earnings' (ibid. p. 23). That shareholders will favour lower retention ratios than managers, furthermore, is suggested by the 'fact' that 'households tend to spend whatever income they can lay their hands on. Households do not save, by and large and on the average, except inadvertently – when their incomes are rising faster than they can adjust their spending' (ibid. p. 22).

With only transient personal saving, it follows that 'households' will hardly be able to offset increases in corporate retentions by reducing their personal saving and/or borrowing. The latter suggestion in particular is supported by 'casual empiricism' which shows that the overwhelming majority of graduate students, a group with good prospects of high future incomes, basically 'limit their borrowing to the expenses of their education and the basic necessities of life' (ibid. p. 35). It follows that 'there is no systematic relationship (specifically no inverse relationship) between corporate saving and personal saving' (Marglin, 1975a, p. 10); i.e. corporate and personal saving are independent.

It is fair, I think, to suggest on the basis of the above that Marglin's position, although better argued, is hardly different from the managerialist one.[3] In particular, along with managerialists and neoclassicals, Marglin appears to deny the potential importance of capitalist control through share-ownership in the process of capital accumulation. It is a virtue of Baran and Sweezy's (1967) viewpoint that (although they themselves accepted the managerialist control idea) they have never gone as far as denying capitalists' existence and/or importance. Although

the special managerial interest in a low pay-out rate does exist and is undoubtedly important [. . .] this makes managers the allies of the very largest stockholders for whom a minimum pay-out rate is also a desideratum. The reason of course is that the very rich save a large part of their incomes in any case, and *it is to their advantage for the corporations in which they own stock to do the savings for them* rather than pay out dividends from which to do their own savings (ibid. p. 47, emphasis added).

It follows that for Baran and Sweezy it is the big shareholders who save within the corporations (parts of which) they own and not the corporations – run by neutral, impartial and impersonal technocrats – who save on behalf of capitalists and workers alike.

Baran and Sweezy's insights were not developed by them as far as an analysis of the substitutability issue. Thus, it can be suggested that all existing analyses on this question are based on an explicit or implicit rejection of the possibility that big shareholders exercise control of the corporations *via* only partial ownership. This possibility we argued in the previous chapter is a very distinct one.

In particular the adoption of our suggestion that it is the capitalists' motivation to accumulate profits that led to the expansion of firms and, as a result, to capitalists' full control of firms, albeit through only partial ownership, offers new insights on the substitutability of saving issue; these result from examining the theoretical validity, or lack thereof, of the managerialist and neoclassical hypotheses in the light of our suggestion of capitalist control.

To illustrate the above, consider the following scenario. In every specific period, say $t - 1$, the controlling capitalists control the profits of the firms, defined in the aggregate to be distributed profits (dividends), plus undistributed profits (retentions), plus rent and interest earned by investment management of the firms' capital. In the same period the group in question decide on their consumption/savings patterns, that is, on the part of the income they own (a proportion of aggregate profits) which they prefer to consume and/or save. Suppose this decision is completed in the same period.

In period t we observe the effects of the completed decision, namely a part of the controlling group's income in the form of savings and the other in the form of consumption. The part saved, however, will have taken the form of personal saving and/or corporate retentions, i.e. business saving.

It follows that, by definition, a part of the observed corporate retentions in every specific period t is the part of the controlling group's income that this group has decided to save within the corporation: i.e. simply a form of the controlling group's savings. The other part of retentions, however, represents the savings within the corporation that the controlling group has decided to make on behalf of the rest of non-controlling shareholders, and it does not necessarily reflect the latters' choice. This important phenomenon arises from the fact that capitalists need only own a proportion of shares in order to control *all* corporate income.

The implication of this is that, regarding the controlling group, actuality is just the realization of their past decisions. Or, in terms of the substitutability issue, the perfect substitution hypothesis is true by definition. This is independent of whether or not capitalists exhibit a preference for corporate retentions. Savings may be mostly done in the form of personal savings rather than corporate retentions, and this will have no effect on the posited perfect substitution between the two. Alternatively, if capitalists do exhibit a preference for retentions, in the limit we may have a situation where all their saving is made within the firms, and personal savings do not exist on their part, except e.g. for transaction purposes. Again the perfect substitution hypothesis will be true. The crux of the matter is that the part of their income that capitalists save within the corporation is the part of their income that they have decided not to consume and/or save in the form of personal savings.

We conclude that corporate decisions, far from being a constraint on the controlling group's preferences, are only a reflection of these preferences.[4] For this group, the neoclassical proposition that corporate decisions are a reflection of individuals' preferences is correct. Not surprisingly either, since it is this group that controls the corporations.[5] The problem with the neoclassical analysis in our framework arises from the fact that capitalists do not control only the income they own, but other people's income too. The behaviour of the non-controlling households, however, may be different.

Generally speaking, non-controlling groups may comprise the vast majority of people: the lower-middle and middle classes such as small shopkeepers and other self-employeds, as well as workers. To the extent that these people do not own shares, the corporate controlling group's policies on retentions have no direct impact on their consumption/saving patterns. If they do own shares, however, corporate retention policies may or may not be desirable from their point of view. Let us assume for the sake of the argument that in a certain period, t, the retention ratio is set to a higher level than the one desired by small-scale shareholders. As a result the latter find themselves with a total level of savings higher than the one they would have chosen if they decided upon the retention ratio. How do they react? Assuming that they are able to 'pierce the corporate veil', that they have sufficient personal savings, and/or that they are able and/or willing to exhaust their possibilities with regard to borrowing, they can either reduce their personal savings by a sufficient amount, or borrow in order to reach their desired level of consumption. Another possible action is to attempt to 'declare their own dividends' by selling all or part of their shares. In doing so, small shareholders will be able to realize the cash they need to restore their consumption levels. Further, they will put pressure on corporate controllers by driving share prices down and perhaps inviting a take-over bid by another group of capitalists.

If any (combination) of the above options is available to, and used by, the non-controlling shareholders, observed retention ratios and/or private saving ratios will be the reflection of a 'consensus' on the part of all shareholders. The neoclassical hypothesis of perfect substitution will be true. Besides assuming a high degree of rationality on the part of small-level shareholders, the validity of the perfect substitution idea is open to criticism from many other angles. First, the possibility of non-positive short-run saving out of small shareholders' truly disposable income cannot be excluded on *a-priori* grounds. In fact, as I will detail later on, this possibility is well in line with the existing evidence for the US and the UK. Borrowing, on the other hand, is not necessarily easy and always accessible. The possibility that low-income households, in particular, may be liquidity-constrained due to 'imperfect' capital markets and the associated difficulties they face in borrowing is a well-accepted one, even within the neoclassical tradition, see e.g. Feldstein (1978), Tobin (1980). That existing small-level shareholders will sell their shares, moreover, is simply not self-evident, for a number of reasons, including transaction costs, particularly important in the case of small lots; tax disadvantages, given that income realized from selling shares will be taxed at a higher rate than retained income; and the uncertainty and volatility of the shares markets, which may result in substantial shareholders' costs if they sell when the market is low.

The above considerations are reinforced by the 'information effect' of dividends, see Wood (1975). When substantial variations are observed in the dividend payments, shareholders may decide to sell their shares. However, a cut in dividends tends to decrease share prices, thus making it a bad time to sell. This makes the process of declaring one's own dividends particularly costly and tends to result in the 'clientele' phenomenon, a situation where 'not only do particular shareholders favour particular companies at a moment of time, but they persist in their favours over considerable periods, sticking to particular shares through thick and thin' (Wood, 1975, p. 37).

The result of all of the above is that, even if existing small shareholders are able to 'pierce the corporate veil', their ability to fully offset corporate retention policies by appropriately adjusting their behaviour may be limited, particularly in the short run, implying less than perfect substitution between corporate retentions and personal saving. Coupled with our analysis of the controlling capitalists' behaviour, the above would suggest imperfect substitution on aggregate, the degree of imperfection depending upon the proportion of shares held by controlling capitalists and the extent to which existing small-level shareholders are able to offset corporate retention policies.

I conclude that the possibility of the existence of a link between corporate retention policies, household choice and financial capital accumulation is a distinct one. It does not require reliance on the assumption that managers control the firms. In fact the adoption of our proposition that capitalists control the firms has this interesting implication – that the neoclassical hypothesis that the above link does not exist is found to be correct for those who exercise control, but incorrect for existing small-level shareholders. Regarding the latter, the managerialist and Marglin's analyses appear to be closer to reality. All three approaches, however, seem to unduly generalize their conclusions to all societal groups.

Although the limited ability of the small-level shareholders to fully offset capitalists' decisions appears in the short run to fit well with observed reality, it may also be plausible to suggest that in the longer run small-level shareholders dissatisfied with the policies of 'their' corporations may eventually sell their shares and perhaps use the realized income to finance current consumption. Alternatively, existing small-level shareholders may simply decide not to add to their existing shareholdings, as their incomes grow. In both the above cases the long-run effect of small shareholders' behaviour would be to endanger the ability of firms to expand through internal financing.

Granted the above, it follows that in the case of direct shareownership the power of the controlling capitalists to raise finance by increasing the retention ratio over time is limited by the ability of small shareholders to eventually sell their shares or choose not to buy new ones. To the extent, moreover, that the advertising and other selling/promotion activities of the firms induce a preference for current consumption in small-level shareholders, the aggregate level of shares held by the latter might be expected to decline, thus defying the ability of the firms to raise finance through this route. In the case of direct shareownership, therefore, Galbraith's presumed ability of the corporate sector to remove the function of capital accumulation from the households, is a very precarious one. This is not the case when shareholding becomes indirect, a phenomenon basically associated with the emergence and growth of occupational pension funds schemes, the 'pension funds revolution'.

The 'pension funds revolution', indirect shareownership and 'social' choice

A new step towards the SOMP has been achieved through the introduction and expansion of occupational pension funds schemes. The stated aim of such schemes is to defer part of the participating employees' income, in order to finance the latters' retirement. Contributions to the schemes are made by both employers and employees and are used by the investment managers of the funds to buy corporate shares, government securities, property, etc., either in the domestic economy or overseas. The total contributions to the funds plus the property income (dividends, rent and interest) earned by the funds minus the benefits paid to employees and the administrative costs of the funds, represent the net inflow of a pension fund. As the participation in a pension fund is usually linked to a life insurance policy, reference is usually made to life assurance and pension funds (LAPF).

In contrast to social security schemes which usually operate on a pay as you go basis, i.e. current contributions are used immediately to finance current benefits, pension funds schemes are normally funded; i.e. the company is required to actually maintain a fund the assets of which should equal the present actuarial value of the employees' anticipated benefits. Since the Second World War, participation in pension funds schemes has increased dramatically, particularly in the US and the UK. In the latter, for example, participation in the schemes was rising steadily after the Second World War and reached a peak in 1967, with around half of the workforce belonging to schemes. This proportion remained stable up to 1979 and increased to around 52 % of total employed people in 1983.[6] Life assurance and pension funds increased from a mere 17 % of personal sector's financial assets in 1962, to 41 % in mid-1985. In the US, Drucker (1976) observed pension funds already owned one-third of all business equity, in the mid-1970s, and the tendency was increasing. In the UK the figure was nearly 29 % in 1985, up from just 3.4 % in 1957.

Two basic explanations were offered for the dramatic growth of pension funds. Green (1982) suggested that the main reason for the schemes was an employers' attempt to increase the loyalty of, and thus their control over, the workforce. In general, it can be suggested that if employers incur information and training costs from employees who leave their jobs 'early', they will have an incentive to discourage potential early leavers. Pension funds schemes can succeed in doing so under certain conditions. If, for example, there is no full transferability of pension funds' rights – defined as the entitlement of the early leavers to their full contributions plus those of their employers and full indexation, i.e. inflation proofing on leaving – employees might be reluctant to leave their jobs early. Much the same applies if pension benefits are measured as a fraction of the last (number of) years' salary – 'final salary schemes'. Finally, if the 'vesting' conditions are such that leaving before retirement implies a loss of pension rights, employees might again be reluctant to change employers to as not to lose such rights.[7] If any of the above conditions exist in reality, then the 'loyalty' of the workforce to their current employers will increase, and labour mobility will be reduced. If, moreover, participation in the schemes is compulsory, i.e. a condition of employment, employees will have no option but to participate in the schemes and be 'loyal' to their employers.

In the UK at least, Green (1982) suggested, most of the above conditions are satisfied; most pension funds schemes are compulsory and strong disincentives to early leavers exist. Further, it would appear that the introduction of the schemes was basically due to the initiatives of the employers, while unions were originally reluctant. All in all, the above would appear to lend support to the 'loyalty of the workforce' hypothesis.

Still, as Rose (1983) observed, the 'loyalty of the workforce' argument is subject to various objections. For example, it disregards potentially more flexible and attractive ways available to employers of purchasing loyalty, and fails to explain why pension schemes began in the Civil Service, i.e. occupations attractive to those employees who valued stability of employment, rather than amongst unskilled workers. Moreover, Drucker (1976) for the US and Minns (1981) for the UK have suggested that both employers and employees favoured the introduction of the schemes, which would appear to tell against Green's suggestions to the contrary.

The second reason advanced to explain the introduction and growth of the funds is their presumed role as a 'saving instrument'. According to this view pension funds, being deferred wages, result in a part of the workers' 'life cycle' income being saved before it actually gets into their hands. This reduces the obvious 'risk' of this income being consumed rather than saved. Further it has the beneficial effect, to the company sector, of putting part of the company finance outside the direct control of the banking system, see Rose (1981). To the extent that increases in pension funds result in a higher part of the workers' income being saved than would be the case in the absence of the pension funds, workers are faced with 'forced saving', see Feldstein (1978), and aggregate financial capital accumulation increases.

There is no obvious reason why the two arguments described above cannot be seen as complementary. A possible scenario is as follows. Employers view pension funds as a means of raising finance without the intervention of the banking system and/or as a means of purchasing workforce loyalty. To achieve their aim they lobby the government to grant preferential tax treatment to the pension funds income. This tends to induce employees to participate in the schemes. Both employers and employees may thus agree to participation in the schemes being compulsory. Moreover, the use by the employers of disincentives to early leavers will tend to ensure the loyalty of the workforce.

It would appear to us that the saving instrument hypothesis is a closer description of reality than the loyalty of the workforce argument. Not only is it not subject to the same criticisms as the latter but it is also consistent with the tendency over the last thirty years for personal shareholding to decline, the very same years when the dramatic growth of the pension funds has taken place, and thus can be seen as a response to it by capitalists. In more general terms, in our framework the introduction and expansion of pension funds can be seen as an attempt on the part of the corporate sector to sustain and even enhance aggregate shareholding and thus business finance through retained profits.[8] Put differently, it can be seen as an attempt to remove the decision to hold shares from the discretion of the household sector and to further disperse share-ownership to those sectors of the population which in the absence of the pension funds schemes might not, and in all probability would not, voluntarily buy shares, i.e. the workers.

Whether increases in pension funds result in increasing financial capital accumulation by restricting the consumption/saving choices of the participating employees depends heavily on the issue of the control of pension funds. If, for example, pension funds are controlled by the participating employees and/or their trustees, it could be suggested that decisions on pension funds investment represent the preferences of all participating employees. This view was favoured by Drucker (1976). In the case of the US, Drucker suggested, the ownership of pension fund shareholding was sufficient to ensure the control of the means of production by US workers. In this sense the 'unseen' pension funds revolution had transformed the US into the first truly socialist country. The first US company to introduce this 'revolution' and thus become the agent of socialism was ... General Motors!

Interesting as they are, Drucker's ideas fail to distinguish between ownership and control of pension funds. In the UK, Minns (1981) attacked Drucker's views and focussed on the control rather than the ownership of the funds. He concluded that around 67% of all pension funds are controlled by the financial institutions which manage them. Even in the case of in-house management, moreover, i.e. the management of the funds internally by the relevant firm, participating employees and their trustees had little say over the investment of 'their' pension funds.

Importantly, the lack of control by participating employees over 'their' funds has this consequence. Most employees are simply not aware of, and thus not interested in, their ownership claims on corporate shares through their pension funds. This casts severe doubt on the neoclassical hypothesis of substitutability between corporate retentions and small shareholders' personal saving: in the case of these shareholders the knowledge of their shareownership (thus any expectation of reaction to changes in the retention ratios of 'their' firms is simply not there. As a result pension funds help to sustain and even enhance aggregate shareholding and at the same time tend to ensure the inability of small shareholders to react to corporate retention decisions by removing from their control (even the knowledge of their ownership claims) on firms' shares. In this sense, pension funds result in a positive link between decisions on corporate retentions and financial capital accumulation.

Besides their indirect impact on financial capital accumulation through their shareholding, pension funds may also have a direct impact through increases in their net inflow. Contrary to its treatment in the official statistics, which view it as personal sector disposable income, the net inflow in pension funds (NILP) is not directly available to the participating employees for consumption, as is the case of corporate retentions. Increases in NILP therefore may result in increasing financial capital accumulation, by restricting the consumption/saving decisions of participating employees.

The above observation has become the subject of debate between the proponents of the neoclassical hypothesis of perfect substitution, and their critics. According to the neoclassical view, as expounded e.g. by Feldstein (1978), undesired changes in NILP may be fully offset by workers' behaviour, thus leaving the personal sector saving to income ratio constant.

The limitations of the above argument are obvious and (some) have been acknowledged by the very same proponents of the perfect substitution idea.[9] To start with, contrary to voluntary small-level shareholders who by virtue of their purchases of shares reveal some ability and desire to save, workers may have no reason or desire to do so. For example, as Feldstein (1978) himself observes, most low-earnings employees may not wish to save for their retirement, simply because they think that their public social security programmes provide them with sufficient retirement income. Such benefits replace 85% or more of their lost income in the US, and the situation appears to be similar in the UK, see Zabalza et al. (1978). Given that, Feldstein suggests: 'Since these individuals would generally find it impossible to borrow against future pension benefits, they are forced to accumulate more for their retirement, than they would otherwise prefer' (Feldstein, 1978, p. 282).

More generally, the awareness by participants of their pension funds rights may be incomplete or underestimated due to uncertainty and illiquidity of pension funds equity. This may tend to result in a low valuation on pension funds rights by participants, who may thus end up with a higher level of total assets than desired. Important, moreover, is the distinction between employees' and employers' contributions. While both represent 'deferred wages', it is not obvious that workers will view them under the same light. In particular, employees may view as theirs only their own contributions. Employers' contributions, after all, never appear on a wage or a salary slip, and as a result they may not give employees the impression that they are paid out of their own money.

The conclusion from the above is that increases in NILP may very well result in directly increasing financial capital accumulation, implying imperfect substitution or even independence between pension funds and employees' personal saving. In addition the idea of complementarity, i.e. that increases in NILP will increase financial capital accumulation by more than the increase in NILP, by leading to increases in personal saving as well, has been advanced by Cagan (1965) and Katona (1965). Cagan justified the possibility of complementarity in terms of what he called the 'recognition effect'. According to this pension fund saving may make participants recognize that a subjectively perceived 'adequate' retirement income, which previously was out of their reach, is now attainable. This will make them save more out of their personal disposable income, in order to attain this retirement income level. Katona, on the other hand, suggested the existence of a 'goal gradient' effect, apparently derived from psychological theories, according to which one intensifies one's effort the closer one is to one's goal. Pension funds saving bring people closer to their target retirement income and thus makes them intensify their efforts to reach this level by increasing their personal saving as well.

On balance, and on the basis of the above, it would be surprising if increases in NILP were fully offset by decreases in workers' personal saving. Thus, the above direct effect of NILP on financial capital accumulation will tend to reinforce the indirect one which operates through the effects of pension fund shareholding on the substitutability between CORE and personal saving.

Capital accumulation and 'social' choice

In the absence of a 'managerial revolution', the existence of differential 'preferences' on the retention and NILP ratios by capitalists on the one hand, and non-controlling shareholders on the other, needs explaining. We suggest here that in a capitalist economy such an explanation can be provided by focussing on the very logic of the process of capital accumulation; in particular, capitalists need to generate potential profits at the production process and be able to realize them by selling their products at a profitable price. This argument is more akin to the Marxist tradition according to which, in capitalist economies, the success or failure of capitalists depends upon their ability to compete. First, with their workers so as to ensure the production to the highest possible level of profits, subject to the subsistence requirements of their workers. Second, with their fellow capitalists, so as to ensure that they appropriate the highest possible share of total profits.

A capitalist who fails to compete in the above framework is sooner or later a non-capitalist. The survival of those left depends upon their ability to compete successfully. In the above sense competition ensures that capitalists will tend to accumulate. This capitalist endeavour will operate under competitive market structures as well as under monopolistic ones, see Mandel (1967a). In particular the emergence of the monopolistic stage of capitalism does not necessarily lead to any qualitative differences as regards the motive to accumulate. The success of monopoly capitalists still depends on their ability to generate profit at the production process and in getting a higher share of it, than other capitalists. What changes is capitalists' ability to collude so as to appropriate a higher level of profits in the exchange process by exploiting the workers in their role as consumers. This may lead to a coexistence of rivalry and collusion betweenn capitalists, see Cowling (1982), a coexistence which in itself can be seen as the result of capitalists' common aim to exploit workers on the one hand, and intercapitalist differences concerning a share of the fruits of exploitation, on the other.

The two types of competition described above can be used to explain the existence I have so far assumed of differential preferences as regards the retention ratio by capitalists on the one hand and non-controlling shareholders on the other. The preference of a high retention ratio by industrial capitalists, for example, can be seen originally in terms of their competition with financial capitalists. This argument underlies the reasoning of Hilferding (1981) and Kalecki (1971). As already pointed out in chapter 2, external borrowing from financial institutions always entails the risk of an industrial capitalist losing control to financiers, and thus it is less desirable for this reason than the retention of one's 'own' profits. For each individual industrial capitalist, therefore, retention of profit is viewed as the safer option and thus 'preferred' to external borrowing. In the aggregate this explains industrial capitalists' 'preferences' for a high retention ratio.

Potential profits, however, cannot be realized as profit unless produced goods are sold at a profitable price. This necessitates the bolstering of consumers' demand through advertising and other selling activities, so as to sell produced goods. The latter, in its turn, tends through a 'demonstration effect', see Duesenberry (1967), to induce a preference for high consumption levels by consumers. As a result, high pay-out rates will tend to be preferred by small-level shareholders so as to satisfy the latters' advertising-induced high consumption needs.

It follows from the above that the capitalists' motive to accumulate and its associated coexistence of rivalry and collusion can explain the existence of differential preferences on retentions by controlling capitalists and non-controlling shareholders. This inverts the underlying causality in the managerial literature which goes from managers' preferences to restricted social choice and financial capital accumulation. In our framework, the dynamics of capital accumulation is the independent variable, which simultaneously determines the preferences of economic 'agents' and, in the particular case of retentions, results in restricted consumption/saving choices of the non-controlling shareholders.

An advertising-induced high preference for small shareholders' consumption, however, may tend to depress the shareholding held by the personal sector. It is here that the introduction and expansion of occupational pension funds schemes becomes a necessity. In this sense the latter can also be seen as the result of capitalists' motive to accumulate, rather than the (exogeneous) preferences of economic agents. The advertising policies of the corporate sector and the fact that state pensions often represent a sizeable proportion of workers' pre-retirement income, may explain the latters' preference for low contributions to LAPF. The ability of financial and/or industrial capitalists to invest NILP profitably (domestically or overseas), on the other hand, may explain their preferences for high contributions to LAPF. A source of intercapitalist conflict in this case arises from the fact that the property income of NILP increases as dividends increase. In the case of pension fund shareholding it is possible that financial institutions in control of the funds may demand higher dividends to increase NILP and invest the latter where they prefer. This would tend to deprive domestic industrial capitalists of internal funds by decreasing the retention ratio. It is unlikely, however, that industrial capitalists will not react to that by, for example, deciding to manage the pension funds themselves, in-house management. Their ability to do so will tend to ensure that the decision on CORE and NILP will be taken jointly by industrial and financial (finance) capitalists. In this sense the 'pension funds revolution' may tend to enhance collusion between capitalists. The needs of finance capital as a whole to accumulate profits will tend to ensure their 'preference' for higher overall retention and NILP ratios than that of the non-controlling shareholders/workers.

In the above scenario, one can also explain why small shareholders buy shares at all, as well as the taxation policies of the state regarding particularly corporate retentions. As Hilferding (1981) suggested, in their attempt to attract other people's money capitalists would attempt to provide some incentives. One such incentive is the payment of a dividend just higher than the prevailing rate of interest. Another is to attempt and obtain a preferential tax treatment of retentions by lobbying the state. Provided the appropriate links between corporate leaders and state officials exist, the above may always be a possibility. In this sense, the existing preferential tax treatment of retentions in most capitalist countries can be seen as the result of the capitalist motive to accumulate and the associated accommodation of this aim by the state authorities. The new element here is that causality runs from capital accumulation to capitalist preference for high retentions to tax concessions, rather than the other way around. Similar also is the case of pension funds. The importance of the above line of thought lies in that it views tax advantages as shaping the preferences of small shareholders' behaviour but by no means capitalists' behaviour as well, as the managerialists (but also Baran and Sweezy, 1967) suggest. The latter instead is viewed in terms of their motive to accumulate profits.

In the light of the above it can be stated that it is not managerial preferences that saved capitalism, by ensuring the continuation of the process of capital accumulation. Rather, it is the capitalists' motivation to accumulate that results in the appearance of the joint stock company, and its associated dispersed share-ownership and restriction of the consumption/saving choices of small-level shareholders. The significance of the pension funds 'revolution', further, does not lie in transforming capitalism to socialism. Rather it lies in allowing capitalists to sustain and enhance aggregate shareholding and thus increase the total level of financial capital accumulation by removing the decision to save from the vast majority of people, the participants in compulsory pension funds schemes.

The existing statistical evidence

Two types of evidence have been used to test the degree of substitutability between different types of saving. First, indirect evidence, obtained by attempting to deduce substitution by observing household saving and/or the constancy or otherwise of the saving to income ratio. Second, direct evidence, obtained by undertaking econometric testing of the hypotheses under consideration.

In the first category proponents of the perfect substitution hypothesis focussed on what is now called the 'Denison's Law'. Denison (1958) observed that in the US, 'the ratio of gross private savings to gross national product was about the same in 1929 and each of the years 1948 through 1953. This ratio continued to hold in 1954, 1955 and on the basis of preliminary estimates, in 1956' (p. 161). The author attributed this stability to the apparent tendency of the ratio of personal saving to Gross National

Product (GNP) to be high when the corporate saving to GNP ratio was low, and vice versa – from which he deduced perfect substitutability between personal saving and corporate retentions. 'Denison's Law' was in more recent years revived in the work of David and Scadding (1974). In line with Denison, the authors observed a long-run tendency of the Gross Private Saving Ratio to GNP in the US to be constant, and attributed their finding to 'ultrarationality', i.e. the presumed ability of households to 'pierce the corporate veil' and offset changes in the saving of the corporations they 'own' by appropriately adjusting their personal saving.

Even disregarding the fact that since the last world war the private saving to GNP ratio has slipped by one point in the US, see Tobin (1980), and two points in the UK, deducing ultrarationality and perfect substitution from the above apparent constancy is a non-sequitur. In particular, one is left wondering why GNP is chosen here as the denominator in preference to the more obvious after-tax private income ratio, see also Marglin (1975). After all, what is really under consideration is the extent to which increases in the after-tax corporate saving to corporate income ratio are offset by reductions in the after-tax personal saving to personal income ratio, which immediately suggests the after-tax private income as the appropriate denominator.

Marglin (1975), on the other hand, sought support for the independence hypothesis by testing for a short-run propensity to consume net personal disposable income equal to one; i.e. zero short-run saving on the part of all households. Marglin used US time series data and defined net personal disposable income to exclude corporate retentions and contractual saving through pension funds. He obtained support for his hypothesis. Similar support for the UK is provided by Kennally (1985), who estimated that the discretionary saving to income ratio was on average very close to zero for the 1973–83 period as a whole.[10]

From the host of other studies on the propensity to consume/save, none is a particularly useful test of the Galbraith–Marglin hypothesis as they include contractual saving, particularly pension funds, in their definition of personal disposable income and thus bias this 'propensity' upwards. Still, Marglin's approach also fails to provide direct evidence for the independence hypothesis. The observation that households do not save out of their net personal disposable income is in itself an insufficient indicator of households' ability to borrow and says nothing about shareholders' ability to declare their dividends; i.e. sell their shares.

It follows that a conclusive answer to the substitutability issue may only be obtained, if at all, by focussing on the direct (econometric) evidence.[11] An attempt along these lines for the case of corporate retentions and personal saving was Modigliani (1970). The author regressed the ratio of corporate saving to private income, on the private saving to private income ratio for 24 countries. In his admission, he failed to produce conclusive results. Lambrinides (1972) undertook a similar study in a slightly different framework for 18 developed countries. The author regressed the organizational saving – i.e. the sum of saving done by private and public corporations plus the saving of the general government – to the national income ratio on the national saving (organizational plus personal) to the national income ratio. When corrected for heteroscedasticity the organizational saving to national income ratio was found to be equal to 0.89, which is insignificantly different from one at the 5% level of a 't'-test. This lends support to the independence hypothesis.

A number of studies focussed on the US time series and gave rise to apparently conflicting results. Feldstein (1973) estimated a consumption function for the 1929–66 period (excluding 1942–47) and included corporate retentions as an additional explanatory variable. He found support for the imperfect substitution hypothesis. In a later study Feldstein (1978) estimated a private saving function and used a longer time series and a more complete specification than in his earlier study. He still obtained support for the imperfect substitution hypothesis but in this case the degree of substitutability was lower than the one found in the 1973 study. Bhatia (1979), moreover reexamined Feldstein's (1973) evidence and found results supportive of the independence hypothesis. Lambrinides (1972) estimated private saving functions and covered the 1919–58 period. He found support for imperfect substitution. Burmeister and Taubman (1969) estimated personal saving functions and included corporate retentions as an additional explanatory variable. The latter was found to be insignificantly different from zero, lending support to the independence hypothesis.

More support for the imperfect substitution hypothesis was obtained in Howrey and Hymans (1978) and Furstenberg (1981). In the former study a personal saving function was used and mixed findings were derived. From five equations reported, two supported the independence hypothesis, two the imperfect substitution hypothesis and one the perfect substitution hypothesis, depending on the definition of the dependent variable and the data period covered in the regression. The authors concluded that their 'results are not in conflict with the proposition that business saving is a nearly perfect substitute for personal saving' (Howrey and Hymans, p. 683). Furstenberg (1981) found results similar to those of Howrey and Hymans, by estimating personal saving and corporate saving functions and then a 'combined run' (a private saving function) including the explanatory variables present in the personal and corporate saving functions.

In the case of the UK time series, only Feldstein and Fane (1973) attempted to test the substitutability between corporate retentions and personal saving. The authors estimated a consumption function for the 1948–69 period and found support for the imperfect substitution hypothesis, in line with Feldstein (1973).

It follows from the above that, in the case of corporate retentions and personal saving, and despite their apparent conflict, all existing studies reject the pure version of the substitutability hypothesis, i.e. that of perfect substitution. Despite the often different estimated regressions, data sets and countries examined, the evidence is on balance suggesting that the existing degree of substitution is closer to the independence than to the perfect substitution hypothesis.

In the case of pension funds, early attempts to test the substitutability hypothesis gave rise to apparently perverse results. Cagan (1965) used US cross-section data and found support for the independence hypothesis and possible complementarity. He attributed this latter possibility to the 'recognition' effect, an idea anticipated by Garvy (1950), 15 years earlier. As Murray (1968) points out, Cagan's sample was not representative of the US population. Still, Katona (1965) used a representative sample of households in the continental US and found support for the complementarity hypothesis, a result he attributed to the 'goal gradient' effect. Munnell (1976) attributed the Cagan–Katona findings to the 'induced retirement effect'. According to that the introduction of pension funds schemes induces individuals to retire earlier than in the absence of the schemes. In order to finance their longer retirement, individuals may decide to save more during their working lives. As a result personal savings increase as well. This does not refute the substitutability hypothesis, but simply implies that the substitution effect is partly offset by the indirect effect on saving of the induced retirement effect. Munnell focussed on the effects of pension funds on 'direct' personal saving and found support for the imperfect substitution hypothesis.

The imperfect substitution hypothesis was also supported by Dicks-Mireaux and King (1983) who used Canadian cross-section data. In the UK as well, the existing cross-section evidence conclusively rejects the perfect substitution hypothesis. Zabalza et al. (1978) found support for the independence hypothesis. Green (1981) used data from the 1953 Oxford Saving Survey and the 1964 Family Expenditure Survey and found support for the complementarity hypothesis. Hemming and Harvey (1983) used a more elaborate approximation of the pension funds variable to that of Green's and used a similar data set. They also found support for the complementarity hypothesis, but concluded that the independence hypothesis was equally sustainable to the complementarity one.

On the time series front, Feldstein (1978) had US data for the 1929–74 period. He attempted to estimate the 'differential' impact of pension funds on personal saving, i.e. the effect of pension funds not already captured in the coefficient of the personal disposable income variable used in the regression which itself incorporated the pension funds variable. He found a positive coefficient but insignificant at the conventional 5% and 10% significance levels. However, he was cautious with this result and suggested that the imperfect substitution hypothesis could not be rejected. In the UK, Threadgold (1978) estimated consumption functions using 1963–77 quarterly data, and included a net inflow in pension funds variable in the regressions. His results were interesting in that they gave support to the imperfect substitution hypothesis between personal saving and employees' contributions to pension funds and the independence hypothesis between employers' contributions and personal saving. This result is intuitively appealing, as it would take a very high degree of (ir)rationality for individuals to consider employers' contributions as theirs, and react to their movements. Finally, Browning (1982) used a similar time series to that of Threadgold's, 1962–79, and found imperfect substitution between gross pension wealth (state plus occupational pension wealth) and saving.

It follows from the above that all existing cross-section evidence conclusively rejects the perfect substitution hypothesis. The same is also true of the time series studies available, save perhaps for Feldstein's study.

It is reasonable I think to conclude, on the basis of the above, that the existing statistical evidence on the substitutability between corporate retentions and/or pension funds, on the one hand, and personal saving on the other, rejects the hypothesis that such substitutability is perfect. In this sense the evidence lends support to the proposition that changes in the corporate retentions and/or the net inflow in pension funds act as a constraint to small-level shareholders and the workers participating in pension funds schemes' consumption/saving patterns and thus result in a higher level of financial capital accumulation. In particular, it is worth emphasizing that the indirect share-ownership by workers through the pension funds 'revolution' appears to restrict the latter's choices in two complementary ways; first through changes in retained earnings and second through changes in the net inflow in LAPF.

CHAPTER 4

The saving function

A necessary condition for the continuation of the process of capital accumulation in a capitalist economy is the availability of saving. Not surprisingly, the question of who 'abstains' from consumption so that financial capital accumulation can take place has assumed prominence in the history of economic thought.

According to the classical economists, the only source of saving was capitalists' profits. Workers were simply not earning enough to save, thus using all of their income to finance their subsistence level of consumption. The inequality in the ownership of the means of production and the associated existence of an owning class and a non-owning class is, according to the classical economists, the key to the accumulation of capital.

The classical view on saving has survived to-date in the writings of Kalecki as well as in the work of some economists in the Marxist tradition.[1] In more recent years, however, a variation of the classical saving function was proposed by the followers of Keynes and became the subject of fierce debate between its proponents and critics. According to this neo-Keynesian Saving Function, both workers and capitalists save, but the proportion of saving out of (capitalists' income) profits is higher than that out of (workers' income) wages. An important reason for that is suggested to be the retention of profit within the corporations.

The neo-Keynesian interest in corporate retention, I suggest, represents a tendency towards a shift of emphasis on the issue of saving from the consumer to the corporation. This is in line with the reasoning of the proponents of the 'managerialist revolution' idea, and has been formalized in the so-called 'Managerialist Saving Function' (MSF). According to this, the dilution of corporate ownership today and its associated assumption that non-shareholder managers control the firms, implies that one should no longer focus on differential 'propensities' between different types of household income, but rather on differential 'propensities' between household income on the one hand and corporate income on the other.

The above distinction is also implicit in the neo-Keynesian writings. Variations of it have been adopted by authors in the Marxist tradition and formalizations of it have been provided by post-Keynesian economists. In this sense the MSF represents a convergence point between a wide spectrum of economic ideologies.

In this chapter we suggest that in its present form the MSF only accounts for the first stage in the dilution of corporate ownership, i.e. direct share-ownership through voluntary shareholding. It thus needs to be extended in order to account for the pension funds 'revolution', and its associated retention of an additional part of (non-controlling) households' income, that of the workers, by the corporate sector. According to this extended MSF, households save out of their discretionary income only, i.e. personal disposable income exclusive of retentions and the net inflow in pension funds, while the last two represent the saving of the corporate sector.

An important implication of the pension funds 'revolution' is that, by retaining a part of workers' income in the form of the net inflow in pension funds (NILP), it casts doubt on the neo-Keynesian view that corporate retention of profit is in itself sufficient to warrant a higher 'propensity' to save profits than wages. For example, the total proportion of the net inflow in pension funds to total wage income can in principle become high enough to result in a higher 'propensity' to save wage income, rather than profit income. For aggregate 'propensities' to be found one should be able to appropriately impute corporate retentions and the net inflow in LAPF to wage and/or profit income, and then proceed to estimate them statistically. In so doing, however, observed proportions would not represent actual 'propensities' but rather an amalgam of actual propensities out of discretionary income, and saving made on households' behalf by the corporate sector.

The MSF and its extended form proposed here are in stark contrast to the neoclassical theory of saving. According to the latter, the level of financial capital accumulation in capitalist economies is determined by the independent decisions of all households, each deliberately and consciously allocating their total (inclusive of retentions and NILP) income/wealth, between present and future consumption. In doing so households view all their income as homogeneous, and thus their personal and corporate saving as full substitutes. In this sense both the MSF and our proposed extension are simple artefacts, arising from the false distinction of household saving in personal and corporate saving.

Our theoretical analysis of the substitutability issue in the previous chapter, and the evidence we marshalled in its favour, would not appear to lend support to the neoclassical views, but rather to our proposed extension of the MSF; a conclusion reinforced by the existing evidence on differential saving 'propensities', and our new evidence provided in this chapter.

Direct share-ownership and the saving function

The idea that different types of income-classes of income recipients may exhibit different patterns of consumption/saving has assumed prominence in the history of economic thought, particularly in the theory of the saving function.

According to the 'Classical Saving Function', e.g. in Marx (1954) and Ricardo (1973), all saving is made out of profits. According to Marx the competition between capitalists and workers as regards the generation of 'surplus value', on the one hand, and the competition between capitalists themselves as to who is going to appropriate a higher portion of this 'surplus value', on the other, ensure the existence of capitalists' endeavour for profits. Ricardo, on the other hand, chose to explain the capitalists' endeavour for profits in terms of their seeking of power and an assumed link between profits and power. Both Marx and Ricardo suggested that current wages will tend not to diverge substantially from the subsistence requirements of the workers, ensuring zero saving on the latter's part. In the Classical Saving Function, capitalists' profits are synonymous with corporate profits, as capitalists are the sole owners of *their* business.

The advancement of capitalism with its entailed improvement in the absolute standards of living of the working class, led to the empirical observation that workers, too, save. This observation was formalized in the neo-Keynesian Saving Function, according to which both capitalists and workers save, but the (capitalists') propensity to save profits is higher than the (workers') propensity to save wages. For Kaldor (1960)

$$S = s_W W + s_\Pi \Pi \qquad 0 \lessgtr s_W < s_\Pi < 1 \tag{1}$$

where S = saving, W = wage income, Π = profit income and s_W, s_Π are the propensities to save W and Π respectively. Kaldor attempted to justify the assumption of a higher propensity to save profits in terms of the presumptions that profits are riskier than wages and that profit income is normally skewed in favour of the relatively wealthier high-income-earning households, see Hacche (1979).[2] Even independently of these two reasons, however, Kaldor (1960) suggested the retention of profit within the corporate sector is sufficient *per se* to justify a differential saving propensities assumption.

In reply to an allegation by his neoclassical critics according to which the differential saving propensities assumption is tantamount to assuming permanent classes of capitalists and workers, see Kregel (1971) for a discussion, Kaldor (1966) elevated the role of corporate retention from a footnote in his original study to the cornerstone of his analysis in the 1966 paper. According to an oft-quoted statement, he has 'always regarded the high saving propensity out of profits as something which attaches to the nature of business income and not to the wealth (or other peculiarities) of the individuals who own property. The high saving propensity attaches to the profits as such, not to the capitalists as such' (1966, p. 310).

Kaldor justified his views in terms of the dilution of corporate ownership. Unlike the nineteenth-century capitalists who owned (and saved in) *their* firms, today's firms are owned by shareholders. The latters' propensity to save out of their personal income need bear little relation to the enterprises they own. If, for example, shareholders tend to consume all their dividends and capital gains, this will help to enhance 'the difference in saving propensities between business income and personal income' (ibid. p. 311).

As was detailed in the previous chapter, Kaldor's concern with diluted share-ownership and its associated shift of emphasis from differential propensities between different *types of household income*, to differential propensities between *household income*, on the one hand, and *corporate income*, on the other, is in the heart of the analyses by Galbraith (1967) and Marglin (1975).[3] The *differentia specifica* of the Galbraith–Marglin hypothesis, is simply that today's world is characterized by producers' sovereignty, rather than consumers' sovereignty and that the advertising and other selling/promotion activities of the firms will result in all shareholders spending *all* their disposable income. In this sense, all savings take the form of corporate retentions in the absence of which capital accumulation would no longer take place.

In an attempt to counter the neoclassical critique that the Kaldorian saving function can only be sustained under the assumption of permanent classes, Kregel (1971) in the post-Keynesian tradition, provided a formalization of Kaldor's and the Galbraith–Marglin views. It is possible, Kregel suggested, that we employ the notion of a mythical property-owning democracy, in which there are no wages class and profits class in the sense that all households draw income from both sources. This democracy can be divided into firms and households and employ managers who are automata with no life function at all, except as corporate decision makers, to run the corporations. In such a world, a differential saving propensities function can still be obtained. It may assume the form,

$$S = s_h(W + (1 - r)\Pi) + r\Pi \quad 0 \leqslant s_h < 1 \tag{2}$$

where r is the retention ratio, and s_h is the common propensity to save disposable household income. If the Galbraith–Marglin hypothesis is true, s_h will be zero and corporate retentions will be the only form of saving.

An alternative, more general version of (2), has been proposed by Cowling (1982), in the Marxist tradition. Cowling considered the thrust of Marglin's arguments convincing, but suggested that 'it would seem to be flying to the face of empirical evidence to suggest that the equilibrium propensity to save out of property income will be the same as out of wage income. It would seem more accurate to suggest that an increase in corporate saving can be expected to raise the aggregate rate of saving, but that a shift from wages to profits will also achieve this, even in the absence of an increase in retentions' (p. 50). In terms of (2) Cowling's suggestion is equivalent to allowing for differential propensities out of W and $(1-r)\Pi$, even in the presence of $r\Pi$. Reasons for doing so, apart from resorting to the empirical evidence, might be the Kaldorian concern with the risky character of profits and the presumption that profits might be skewed towards the wealthy.

All the above cases may be seen as variations on the same theme, equation (2). The tendency towards this convergence of the above ideologically broad spectrum of economic theorists received early notice in Lambrinides (1972). He suggested that, contrary to Kaldor's intentions, the latter's propositions in the 1966 paper should not be viewed as a justification of equation (1), which rather should be replaced by 'the managerial saving function which considers private savings to be a function *inter alia* of the division of after tax private income between households and privately owned corporations' (p. 110).

The 'Managerialist' Saving Function and the 'pension funds revolution'

The convergence on the MSF is *not* the necessary result of the assumption that managers control the firms. Rather it is the direct product of the tendency towards the socialization of the ownership of the means of production (SOMP) and the assumption/observation of minority control over publicly 'owned' corporations. The MSF is broadly in line with our analysis so far, according to which a controlling subset of the owners (capitalists) saves in the form of corporate retentions part of their income, but also part of other people's money over which they have control.[4]

Still in its form (2) the MSF fails to account for the impact of the pension funds 'revolution' on the dilution of corporate ownership and the issue of saving. It thus needs extending in this direction. Through the workers' and employers' contributions to the pension schemes and the property income earned by the pension funds shareholding and other investment, an increasingly higher part of total workers' income is taken away from their direct control in the form of the difference between the total income and expenditure of the schemes, the net inflow in pension funds (NILP). Similarly to the case of corporate retentions, NILP is retained in each period by the corporate sector in order to finance next period's investment. In this sense NILP is not available to workers for consumption and in an accounting sense it represents a net addition to the saving of the corporate sector.

Formally, if p represents the part of total wage income retained by the corporate sector in the form of NILP, then workers will only be receiving in each period a proportion of their aggregate income $(1-p)W$. Substituting the latter in (2), gives rise to the extended form of the MSF, as

$$S = s_h[(1-p)W + (1-r)\Pi] + pW + r\Pi \quad 0 \leqslant s_h < 1. \tag{3}$$

As in the case of the MSF, if the Galbraith–Marglin hypothesis is true, $s_h = 0$ and the only form of saving is that of the corporate sector's. The difference now being that equation (3) includes pW as well as $r\Pi$. Similarly, the implied restriction in (3) that the propensity to save $(1-p)W$ is equal to that of $(1-r)\Pi$ can be tested by, for example, allowing for different coefficients of these variables.

An implication of (3) is that for a sufficiently high NILP and p, the aggregate proportion of W saved may be equal to or higher than that out of Π. This casts doubt on the Kaldorian proposition that corporate retention *per se* suffices to establish the differential saving propensities assumption implied in (1). The latter hypothesis can only be tested directly by regressing aggregate saving on W and Π.

A potential limitation of the MSF and our proposed extension here is that they implicitly assume that personal and corporate saving are independent of each other. Alternatively it is assumed that (at least some) households, the ultimate owners of the corporate sector, do *not* take into account their ownership claims on corporate profits and pension funds when forming their consumption/saving decisions. This assumption is in stark contrast to the neoclassical theory of Life Cycle saving, see e.g. Ando and Modigliani (1963). According to this theory households are taken to be rational intertemporal utility maximizers, trying to smooth their consumption throughout their life cycle by saving mainly for retirement purposes during their working lives and then dissaving during their retirement. In doing so, households are able to 'pierce through the corporate veil', i.e. they consider all income they own as theirs, and thus all types of their saving as perfect substitutes. It follows that what appears *ex-post* to be differential propensities between corporations and households, is a simple reflection of all households' *ex-ante* decisions. Both the MSF and our proposed extension here are simple artefacts. They arise from the false distinction of what simply represents household saving into corporate and personal ones; see, however, Bliss (1976) for some critical remarks on this theory from within the neoclassical tradition.

The important issue of substitutability was not considered by Kaldor and Kregel. In this sense the retention of profit idea does not fully resolve the issue of differential propensities, even in the absence of pension funds. In particular, if the perfect substitution hypothesis is true on aggregate, both the MSF and our proposed extension here break down.

The existing empirical evidence

The only attempt to test directly the MSF is Lambrinides (1972). Set out in the framework of the Life Cycle Hypothesis (LCH), the author found support for the idea that corporate retained earnings and disposable personal sector income are imperfectly substitutable by using US time series data, and independent by using international cross-section data. Although the time series evidence did not support either of the two extreme hypotheses, perfect substitution or independence, the author considered his findings as being closer to, and thus supportive of, the MSF, as opposed to the LCH.

Two overlapping and complementary types of existing evidence have implications on our proposed extension of the MSF. First, tests of substitutability between corporate retained earnings and/or pension funds on the one hand, and personal saving on the other. Second, tests on differential propensities between different types of personal (or private) sector wage and profit income.

The empirical studies in the first category have recently proliferated due basically to economists' concern with testing the LCH and/or the related issue of the impact of 'contractual' saving, retentions and pension funds, on capital accumulation. Our detailed survey of this evidence in the previous chapter leads to the conclusion that on balance the evidence lends support to our treatment of corporate retentions and pension funds in (3), as opposed to the alternative implications of the LCH. It thus casts doubt on the validity of the vast majority of orthodox neoclassical studies on the consumption/saving function, see Ferber (1973) and more recently Wallis (1979) for surveys. All such studies make an uncritical use of the official statistics which define personal sector disposable income to include the net inflow in pension funds (NILP) but not corporate retentions, and do not include the last two as separate explanatory variables in their regressions. In doing so these studies effectively assume that NILP is a perfect substitute for personal saving but that corporate retentions are independent from personal saving. Further they assume that the 'propensity' to save total wage income (inclusive of NILP) is equal to the propensity to save personal sector profit income (i.e. exclusive of retentions). Combined with the assumption that the latter are independent of personal saving, the above lend indirect support to the 'Kaldorian' hypothesis, (1), and the MSF and assume on *a priori* grounds that our proposed treatment of pension funds is wrong; an assumption rejected by the studies which explicitly tested it.

In the second category, a number of studies attempted to test directly for differential saving 'propensities' out of personal (or private) sector (disposable) income. From the studies which focussed on personal sector disposable shares, the first one we are aware of is the well-known work by Brown (1952) on the role of 'habit persistence' in consumer's behaviour. Brown used Canadian time series data and distinguished between two types of disposable income shares in his consumption function; wage income consisting of after-tax wages and contributions from the central government to the households (what is usually viewed as the 'social wage'), and profit income, i.e. after-tax dividends, rent, interest and income from self-employment. The implied short-run marginal 'propensities' to save wage income and profit income were 40% and 70% respectively.

A similar exercise was undertaken for the US and UK time series by Klein and Coldberger (1955) and Klein *et al.* (1961) respectively. As in Brown, both studies found support for the differential saving 'propensities' assumption but their obtained 'propensities' were of lower magnitude. In the case of Klein *et al.*, for example, the long-run marginal 'propensities' were 56% and 83% for wage and profit income respectively. More recently, Surrey (1970) used UK time series and obtained 'equilibrium propensities' to save personal sector wage and profit income of the order of 15% and 40% respectively, still in line with the differential 'propensities' assumption. Holbrook and Stafford (1971), however, used US cross-section data and failed to detect any differences between the 'propensity to save labour income (excluding transfers) and profit income. Taylor (1971) used US time series and found a higher propensity to save labour income than property income, but not significantly so. Blinder (1975) also used US time series and found no evidence for differential saving 'propensities' out of personal sector shares. Finally, Arestis and Driver (1980) used UK time series and found a small difference between the proportions of labour and property income saved; of 60% and 70% respectively in the short run.

It appears reasonable to conclude on the basis of the above that the direct evidence on differential 'propensities' out of *personal sector* shares is not inconsistent with the idea that such 'propensities' differ little or not at all.[5] This 'proves' what is normally assumed in the orthodox neoclassical literature and in this sense it provides more indirect support to the MSF given the additional assumption in all the above studies that corporate retentions and personal savings are independent. The substantial existing evidence that the latter hypothesis is closer to reality than its alternative of perfect substitutability reinforces the above conclusion.

It follows from the above that focussing only on personal sector income shares does not provide a direct test of the 'Kaldorian' hypothesis and the MSF. Moreover, the apparent tendency of the 'propensities' to save out of personal sector income shares to be equal, is the result of the increasing importance of corporate retained earnings. It has long been observed that as the proportion of private income retained within the corporate sector increases, an apparent equalization of the income distribution statistics will tend to be observed, see Dobb (1958) and Brittain (1966). The latter author, in particular, examined the role of restrictions in the dividend payments of the corporate sector on the income distribution statistics. He suggested that

Since most studies of individual income distribution do not impute corporate saving to individual stockholders, the fall in the dividend pay-out ratio was reflected in these studies as a levelling effect on the distribution of income ... This indication that the restriction of dividends by corporations ... played a significant role in the apparent equalization of individual incomes clouds the meaning of the income distribution statistics (ibid. p. 6).

Related to the above is also the tendency towards an equalization of the saving 'propensities' out of personal sector income shares. It follows that consistent direct tests of the 'Kaldorian' hypothesis (1) and the MSF can be obtained by including corporate retentions in the definition of profit income, or as a separate explanatory variable in the consumption/saving function *along with* disposable personal sector (shares of profit and wage) income.

The first empirical study to define retentions as profits is Kalecki (1971), first published in 1933. Kalecki estimated a profits equation using US time series. He deduced a proportion of profit income saved – the term propensity is not used by Kalecki – equal to 75%, from an early version of the multiplier. His estimates, however, were based on the assumption of zero saving out of workers and thus they still constitute only indirect support for the 'Kaldorian' hypothesis.

Kalecki's lead was followed by Klein (1950). He estimated a consumption function which included both wage income and profit income, the latter inclusive of retentions *à la* Kalecki. Thus Klein's study constitutes the first direct and consistent test, published six years before the 'Kaldorian' hypothesis was proposed, of the 'Kaldorian' hypothesis. It might be fair therefore to name the hypothesis in question Kleinian! Titles apart, Klein's findings supported the 'Kaldorian' hypothesis. Obtained short-run 'propensities' to save profit income and wage income were of the order of 75% and 20% respectively.

More support for the 'Kaldorian' hypothesis, tested by including corporate retention in profit income, was found by Ando and Modigliani (1963) and Modigliani and Tarantelli (1975), using US and Italian data respectively. In both studies the proportion of aggregate profit income saved was found to be higher than that of wage income, in the latter study, for example, the respective proportions were of the order of 60% and 15%. The authors attributed their results to the idea that profit income is a (poor) proxy for the more appropriate (according to their 'Life Cycle' hypothesis) variable, wealth, as well as to special characteristics of the Italian economy in the second study.

Burmeister and Taubman (1969) also found support for the 'Kaldorian' hypothesis and the MSF by using US time series. They adopted a 'safe' versus 'risky' distinction for personal sector income shares, i.e. wages and salaries, and rent and interest on the one hand, and dividends plus self-employment income on the other. Corporate retentions were included as an additional explanatory variable. The proportion of 'risky' income saved was found to be higher than that of 'safe' income, but never significantly so, in line with the findings of most other studies which focussed on personal sector shares only. The retained earnings variable, however, was found to be totally saved, thus lending support to the idea of a higher proportion saved out of risky (inclusive of retentions) income than that of safe income.

All in all, the above discussion suggests that both the existing indirect and direct evidence lend support to the 'Kaldorian' hypothesis. They also emphasize the crucial role that corporate retained earnings play when the hypothesis is tested; the exclusion of retentions from profits appears to reject the 'Kaldorian' hypothesis while its inclusion lends confident support to it.

As in the case of the orthodox neoclassical literature on the consumption/saving function, these direct tests of the 'Kaldorian' hypothesis and the MSF include the net inflow in pension funds in their definition of (wage) income. This is equivalent to assuming that pension funds and saving out of wage income are perfectly substitutable, a hypothesis the validity of which should be tested rather than assumed. In this sense all the above studies do not test my proposed extension of the MSF. The existing evidence that pension funds and personal sector saving are not perfect substitutes would appear, moreover, to cast doubt on the above treatment of pension funds and thus lend indirect support to my proposed extension.

It appears sensible to conclude on the basis of the above that the existing evidence lends indirect support to my proposed extension of the MSF. The evidence, moreover, on the Galbraith–Marglin hypothesis surveyed in the previous chapter would lead us to believe that the restricted version of the extended MSF, arising from the assumption that the overall household propensity to save discretionary personal disposable income is zero, is correct.

An attempt to test the above hypotheses directly in a common framework is Pitelis (1985). This study used postwar UK time series data, 1951–81, and tested the extended version of the MSF, equation (3), namely the propensity to save personal discretionary income (exclusive of retentions and pension funds), as well as the effects of the latter two on other saving, the substitutability hypothesis of saving. Only limited substitution was found between corporate retentions/pension funds and discretionary personal saving. The data, moreover, did not reject the Galbraith–Marglin hypothesis that the 'propensity' to save discretionary household income is zero. The household sector as a whole was found to save only out of the *change* in their discretionary personal income, lending support to earlier similar findings for the US by Marglin (1975). The importance of this finding lies mainly in that it suggests that increases in corporate retentions/pension funds add *fully* to the existing level of financial capital accumulation. Moreover, the limited substitutability found would suggest that in the absence of corporate saving the aggregate level of financial capital accumulation in capitalist countries might be well below its current level. This supports our theoretical analysis in the previous chapter and provides a formalization of it in the form of equation (3).

The extended MSF is not necessarily incompatible with the classical saving function or the latter's neo-Keynesian version. In principle, one can attempt to identify and impute appropriately, corporate retentions and pension funds in wage and/or profit income, and thus estimate the proportions of aggregate wage and profit income shares saved. In this case, however, the obtained proportions will, in our framework, *not* represent actual 'propensities', but an amalgam of actual propensities out of discretionary personal income shares, corporate saving on behalf of the households and (depending on the specification) 'transient' saving out of households' changing discretionary personal incomes. The term 'propensity' in this framework appears to be misleading as it implies that households have full control of their total income.

A clear implication of our analysis in the last three chapters is that the validity of both the MSF and its proposed extension here does not rely on assumptions regarding who controls today's corporations. Rather, it is in line with any type of minority control of the corporations combined with the existence of diluted share-ownership and the associated potential existence of non-controlling shareholders. Diluted share-ownership and its associated possibility of minority (in our framework, 'capitalist') control of the corporations is the direct result of the appearance of the joint-stock company and its associated tendency towards the socialization of the ownership of the means of production. The latter represent a stage in capitalist development defined here as 'Corporate Capitalism'. In this sense it may be more appropriate to define our proposed extension of the MSF as the Corporate Capitalism Saving Function (CCSF).

New evidence

In summary form, the hypothesis we want to test here is that capitalist control over non-controlling shareholders' income results in different consumption/saving patterns of the above two societal groups. Capitalists regard all their income as homogeneous and thus their personal and corporate saving as full substitutes. Non-controlling shareholders, on the other hand, cannot fully account for their ownership claims on income they do not control, when taking their consumption/saving decisions. It follows that on aggregate corporate saving – retentions and pension funds – are not fully substitutable with non-controlling households' personal saving and thus have a positive impact on private saving – financial capital accumulation. Alternatively stated, the above imply that the aggregate propensity to save out of households' disposable income is lower than that out of corporate retentions and pension funds.

Formally the above can be written as:

$$PRSA_t = a_1 NWI_t + a_2 NPI_t + a_3 NILP_t + a_4 CORE + u_t \qquad (4)$$

where $PRSA$ is S in (3) and stands for private saving,
NWI is $(1-p)W$ and stands for Net Wage Income,
NPI is $(1-r)\Pi$ and stands for Net Profit Income,
$NILP$ is pW, i.e. the Net Inflow in Life and Pension Funds,
$CORE$ is $r\Pi$, i.e. Corporate Retained Earnings,
t is a time subscript, and it is assumed that
$u \sim NI(0, \sigma^2)$, i.e. u is an error term distributed normally with a zero mean and constant variance.

The CCSF, (3), implies the following restrictions on (4):

$$0 \leqslant a_1 = a_2 = s_h < a_3 = a_4 = 1.$$

The restriction $0 = a_1 = a_2 = s_h$ is implied by the Galbraith–Marglin hypothesis. That $a_3 = a_4 = 1$ follows from the fact that, in the CCSF, pW and $r\Pi$ appear without a coefficient. With a coefficient added as in (4) the

CCSF can be taken to be closer to reality than its rival LCH, for as long as the less-stringent restriction $s_h < a_3 \lesseqgtr a_4$ holds true.

In their present form equations (3) and (4) are not designed for estimation purposes and are probably too simplistic to capture the generation process of the data used. This necessitates the derivation–use of an appropriate estimated form of the consumption/saving function, to encompass our propositions in the previous and the present chapter. Such an estimated form, moreover, in itself presupposes a theory of consumption/saving.

A number of theories have been proposed to describe the consumption/saving behaviour of households. The most well-known of them are the Life Cycle Hypothesis (LCH) of Ando and Modigliani (1963), the Adaptive Expectations/Permanent Income (AE/PI) Hypothesis primarily associated with Friedman (1957), the Houthakker–Taylor (H–T, 1970) Hypothesis and the 'Error Correction' model of consumption, first proposed by Marglin (1975) and more recently extended and popularized in Davidson et al. (1978).[6] Less elaborate but also well known are the Partial Adjustment (PA) and the Simple Lag/Habit Persistence (SL/HP) hypothesis of consumption, the latter originally advanced by Brown (1952). The theoretical arguments underlying the above models are by now common ground in the consumption/saving literature, see e.g. Ferber (1973) and Wallis (1979) for surveys, and we will not repeat them here. Instead we will focus on the estimated forms of all these hypotheses. In particular we show in the Appendix to this chapter that all the above theories of consumption/saving can lead to the same 'general' estimated equation of household saving which expresses household disposable saving as a function of the change in household disposable income and households' previous period's saving, i.e.

$$S_t = d_1 \, \Delta Y_t + d_2 S_{t-1} \tag{A}$$

where S and Y are disposable saving and income respectively, and Δ denotes the first difference, i.e. $\Delta Y = Y_t - Y_{t-1}$. Given its generality, (A) can be used as a framework for testing our hypotheses-propositions of the previous and the present chapter, without being subject to the 'criticism' of adhering to a particular theory.

Still, the above 'generality' of (A) is based on the assumption of the adoption of a common definition of S and Y by all theories. Such consistency, however, is not met with in practice. The LCH, for example, has been associated with the use of private (personal plus corporate) S and Y, implying that all types of saving are perfect substitutes, see Modigliani (1975). The H–T model, on the other hand, is usually tested by using personal sector S and Y, i.e. exclusive of corporate retentions, which assumes that personal saving and corporate retentions are independent, but that pension funds and personal saving are perfect substitutes, see Taylor (1971), Taylor and Weiserbs (1972). Most other theories have been cryptic on this matter and empirical research often focusses on the official statistics which use the same convention as in the H–T model. Given, however, that the adopted definition of S and Y incorporates theoretical propositions, the latter should be tested rather than simply be assumed.

The focus of the above theories on household behaviour implies that one should exclude from the definition of disposable Y and S income which households do not directly control, most notably corporate retentions and pension funds. In our framework, in particular, the last two should be excluded from the definition of the disposable Y and S of the non-controlling households, but included in the case of capitalists.[7] Such disaggregated data is not available in practice. Still, there are reasons to believe that the use of a definition of household disposable income and saving exclusive of *all* retentions and NILP can be viewed as a close approximation of the saving and income of the non-controlling sectors of the population. As Williamson (1964) held, for the case of managers, it is plausible to suggest that controlling capitalists will tend to both *consume and save* within the corporation. Saving will take the form of corporate retentions and consumption the form of 'expense accounts', perquisites, etc. Evidence that corporate leaders tend to consume in this way abound in the industrial economics literature, see e.g. Aaronovitch and Sawyer (1975), and Cowling (1982). The part of capitalist income consumed this way does not appear in the official household saving-income accounts. It follows that household income and saving exclude parts of, or perhaps even all of, the income and saving of those who are more likely to be the big savers anyway – capitalists. This leaves us with a more homogeneous subject to deal with; in the limit consisting of non-controlling households only.

Given the above, we ask the following questions regarding the consumption/saving behaviour of the broadly homogeneous household sector. First, what part of their disposable income do they save? Second, to what extent to they take into account income they 'own' but over which they have no direct control, i.e. corporate retentions and NILP? Further, since the last two represent different types of income, do such (and/or other) differences in types of incomes result in different proportions of them being saved? Testing the above questions is tantamount to simultaneously testing all hypotheses discussed and/or proposed in the previous and the present chapter; the 'Kaldorian' saving function (1), the MSF (2), the CCSF (3), the Galbraith–Marglin hypothesis, and the critique to them by the LCH, all in a common framework.

For estimation we use the relatively unexplored UK data. They are annual and cover the 1952–84 period. From them, the Personal Sector Disposable Income (PSDI), Corporate Retained Earning (CORE) and Consumers Expenditure (C) series were taken from the Economic Trends Annual Supplement (ETAS), 1985, and the National Income and Expenditure, Blue Book, 1985. The NILP series was provided to the author by Mike Sherring at the Central Statistical Office. All series are after tax and before providing for depreciation, stock appreciation and additions to tax reserves. Constant 1980 prices have been obtained by using the 1980 Implied Consumers Expenditure Deflator (ICED), obtained from the ETAS, 1985.

Given that the official definition of PSDI includes all contributions to LAPF, rather than the benefits only paid from LAPF to households, we subtracted NILP from PSDI to obtain a measure of the Net Personal Disposable Income (NPDI) of the households. Following conventional national income accounting, NPDI is thus defined as:

$$NPDI = (W + S) + FP + EC + CCG + DIV + RE$$
$$+ INT + SEY - HTAX - HCSS - NILP$$

where $(W + S) =$ Wages and Salaries inclusive of contributions to LAPF
$FP =$ Pay to the National Forces
$EC =$ Employers' Contributions, inclusive of contributions to LAPF
$CCG =$ Contributions to Households from the Central Government
$DIV =$ Dividends
$RE =$ Rent
$INT =$ Interest
$SEY =$ Income from Self-Employment
$HTAX =$ Taxes to Households
$HCSS =$ Households Contributions to Social Security.

As we are interested in disposable income, the exclusion of HTAX and HCSS from NPDI is straightforward. Benefits, however, paid by social security to households are disposable to the latter and thus included in NPDI. The exclusion of NILP (contributions to, minus benefits from, LAPF) ensures that, similarly to the case of social security, only benefits paid from LAPF are included in NPDI. Subtracting C from the latter will give the Net (of NILP) Personal Saving (NPS) of the households.[8]

The private sector is defined as the sum of the personal and corporate sector. It follows that the disposable Private Sector Income (PRI) will consist of PSDI plus Corporate Retentions (CORE), given that the other part of Corporate Income, Dividends, is already included in PSDI. In this sense Private Saving (PRSA) is PRI minus C and comprises the sum of NPS, NILP and CORE. The measure of CORE adopted here is gross of depreciation allowances, see chapter 5.

In its present form (A) incorporates a number of assumptions-restrictions. First, that the household propensity to save out of NPDI is zero in that households save out of the change only of their NPDI.[9] Further, that the above is true for both the wage and profit income parts of NPDI and also that the proportions saved out of the changing Net Wage Income (NWI) and Net Profit Income (NPI) shares are equal to each other. Second, that the household sector does not take account of CORE and NILP when forming their consumption/saving decisions.

The above assumptions-restrictions may be (im)plausible, thus they need to be tested rather than assumed. This can be done by starting from the most unrestricted version of our 'general' saving function and then following a 'general to specific' approach, see Harvey (1981), in order to test the implied restrictions and thus derive statistically the equation which provides the most parsimonious description of our data.[10] In terms of the terminology adopted in equation (4), we can thus write (A) as:

$$NPS_t = b_0 + b_1 NWI_t + b_2 NWI_{t-1} + b_3 NPI_t + b_4 NPI_{t-1}$$
$$+ b_5 NILP_t + b_6 CORE_t + b_7 NPS_{t-1} + v_t. \qquad (5)$$

The restrictions implied from (A.1) on (5) are:

$$0 = b_5 = b_6 < b_1 = -b_3 = b_2 = -b_4 < 1.$$

The constant term b_0 is included in (5) in order to test for the existence of a subsistence level of consumption à la Keynes (1936) (in which case the constant should be negative and significantly different from zero) as opposed to the LCH assumption of homotheticity of the consumption function, from which a zero constant is implied.

The 'whiteness' of the error term above is an assumption. Given the presence of a Lagged Dependent Variable (LDV) in (5), if this assumption does not hold, the presence of the LDV will ensure biased and inconsistent Ordinary Least Squares (OLS) estimates. The traditional Durbin–Watson (DW) statistic for first-order autocorrelation in this framework will be biased towards indicating no autocorrelation, necessitating the use of an alternative means of autocorrelation testing.

The NWI and NPI shares in (5) are derived by adopting on NPDI the conventions established in the classic Klein and Goldberger (1955) and Klein et al. (1961) studies. Thus we define Net Wage Income as

$$NWI = (W + S) + FP + EC + CCG - WTAX - WCSS - NILP$$

where $WTAX$ = Taxes to Wage Income defined as above, and
$WCSS$ = Social Security Contributions out of Wage Income.

Net Profit Income will be

$$NPI = DIV + RE + INT + SEY - TAX - CSS$$

where TAX = Taxes to Profit Income defined as above, and
CSS = Contributions to Social Security out of Profit Income.

Data on taxes and social security contributions out of NWI and NPI were obtained from various issues of the Blue Book.

Conventional as they may be, the above distinctions of NWI and NPI are not free of criticisms. In particular it can be suggested that part (or all) of salaries is in fact profit rather than wage income, see Cowling (1982). Similarly, part (or all) of the contributions from the central government to households such as rebates to employers from redundancy funds and/or grants to universities could be considered as 'social profits' rather than social wages, see e.g. O'Connor (1973).[11] On the other hand, part of SEY may be viewed as an imputed wage of the self-employed rather than profits, see Modigliani (1970). Unfortunately, sufficiently disaggregated data to account for all the above do not exist. It is convenient, however, that the effects of the first two issues above move in the opposite direction to that of the third and may tend to cancel each other out. More importantly the above issues do not bear directly on our attempt to test the CCSF. For the purposes of the latter the more important subdivision is that between household disposable income, on the one hand, and household claims on corporate income on the other.

Given the problems associated with the presence of the LDV in (5), we estimate the latter here by first assuming that the error term is a first-order autoregressive scheme (AR1) of the form, $v_t = \rho v_{t-1} + u_t$, where u is a serially independent disturbance with zero mean. We then attempt to obtain $\hat{\rho}$ by using a Maximum Likelihood (ML) Iterative Technique, specifically designed to do so. When $\hat{\rho}$s are found to be significantly different from zero we report the ML estimates. When they are insignificant, we reestimate the regressions with OLS and report the latter estimates.[12]

On estimation, equation (5) gave:

$$NPS_t = -6876.60^* + 0.24^* NWI_t - 0.14\, NWI_{t-1} + 0.72^* NPI_t$$
$$(-2.07)\qquad(2.35)\qquad\quad(1.35)\qquad\qquad(2.60)$$

$$-0.61^* NPI_{t-1} - 0.72\, NILP_t + 0.03\, CORE_t$$
$$(-2.39)\qquad\quad(-1.18)\qquad\quad(0.33)\qquad\qquad\qquad (6)$$

$$+0.58^* NPS_{t-1} - 0.21 v_{t-1} + u_t$$
$$(2.83)\qquad\qquad(-1.07)$$

$$\bar{R}^2 = 0.8819 \quad SSE = 377 \times 10^{11}.$$

Equation (6) appears to be well specified. The coefficients of all (types of) NPDI variables have the expected signs, the explanatory power of the equation is reasonably high and no first-order autocorrelation appears to exist. The coefficients of the NILP and CORE variables are insignificantly different from zero, lending support to the hypothesis that corporate and personal saving are independent.

Imposing on (6) the restrictions that the coefficients of the current and lagged NWI and NPI are equal, gives equation 1.1 in Table 1. An F-test accepted the restrictions at the 5% level.

The restriction that the coefficients of NPDI is equal to minus that of NPDI was imposed on 1.1 and gave rise to 1.2 in which the change in NPDI affects saving. The restriction was accepted. In both 1.1 and 1.2 the coefficient of the NILP variable is insignificantly different from zero as in (6). The coefficient of CORE, however, is positive and significantly different from zero at the 10% and 5% significance levels of a two-tailed 't'-test in 1.1 and 1.2 respectively. This lends support to the idea of a small degree of complementarity between CORE and NPS.

In all (6), 1.1 and 1.2 the coefficients of CORE and NILP are close to each other. Restricting them to be equal gives 1.3 in Table 1. The restriction is accepted. The coefficient of the resulting variable Corporate (or Contractual) Saving (COSA) is very small and insignificantly different from zero at the 5% level, albeit significant at the 10% level. When restricted to be equal to zero, equation 1.4 resulted. The restriction was accepted at the 5% level of an F-test. It follows that 1.4 is our preferred equation so far. It appears not to suffer from first-order autocorrelation. Further, a Lagrange Multiplier (LM) test for up to fourth-order autocorrelation and misspecification, see Harvey (1981), was significant at the 5% level of a X^2-test, but not at the 2.5% level. It follows from 1.4 that NPS is only affected by its past value and the change in NPDI, implying independence between COSA and NPS.

An alternative, but equivalent to the above way of testing the above hypotheses is to include NILP and CORE both in the definition of the dependent variable, which now becomes Private Saving (PRSA), and as additional explanatory variables in the regression. Doing that in equation 1.4 gives rise to 1.5. This equation exactly replicates 1.2 save that now the coefficients of NILP and CORE are equal to one plus their coefficients in 1.2. In this case the independence hypothesis is supported if the coefficients of CORE and NILP are equal to one. Imposing on 1.5 the restriction that the coefficients of NILP and CORE are equal gives rise to 1.6, which replicates the results of 1.3.[13] The use of this exercise lies in that, despite their formal equivalence to 1.2 and 1.3, equations 1.5 and 1.6 measure the total effect of NILP and CORE on PRSA rather than NPS, therefore giving us a direct test of the CCSF.[14]

Table 1. *Tests of the Corporate Capitalism Saving Function. Annual UK data: 1952–84*

Eqn No.	Dependent variable	Constant	$\Delta NPDI_t$	$NPDI_t$	$NPDI_{t-1}$	$NILP_t$	$CORE_t$	$COSA_t$	NPS_{t-1}	$\bar{R}^2$	SSE	$\hat{\rho}$
1.1	NPS_t	−2771.67 (−1.11)		0.33* (3.85)	−0.31* (−3.47)	−0.39 (1.40)	0.12† (1.99)		0.95* (5.04)	0.9304	397×10^{11}	−0.33† (−1.78)
1.2	NPS_t	−1151.32* (−2.05)	0.34* (4.02)			−0.30 (−1.50)	0.13* (2.45)		1.04* (6.43)	0.9370	402×10^{11}	−0.38* (−2.16)
1.3	NPS_t	−1439.77† (−1.98)	0.22* (2.92)					0.08† (1.80)	0.74* (5.66)	0.8783	440×10^{11}	−0.15 (−0.80)
1.4	NPS_t	−327.64 (−0.83)	0.30* (4.41)						0.95* (14.64)	0.8693	489×10^{11}	−0.18 (−1.02)
1.5	$PRSA_t$	−1151.27* (−2.05)	0.34* (4.02)			0.70* (3.43)	1.13* (21.05)		1.04* (6.43)	0.9958	402×10^{11}	−0.38* (−2.16)
1.6	$PRSA_t$	−1439.72† (−1.98)	0.22* (7.92)					1.08* (23.93)	0.74* (5.66)	0.9915	440×10^{11}	−0.15 (−0.80)

't' ratios in parentheses.
Δ denotes the first difference.
* denotes significance at the 5% level.
† denotes significance at the 10% level.

It can be concluded from the above that our results support the idea that non-controlling households do not take into account their ownership claims on income they do not control, when forming their consumption/ saving decisions. The latter in turn implies that NILP and CORE positively affect the existing level of financial capital accumulation. This lends support to our proposed CCSF, and casts doubt on the implications of the LCH.

It has been found so far that non-controlling households do not save out of the *level* of their NPDI but rather out of the *change* only of the latter; this implies that the propensity to save NPDI as a whole, and thus the propensity to save NWI and NPI, are equal to each other and both equal to zero. An alternative but equivalent way to 1.1 of testing the above hypothesis is by including NWI and NPI as additional explanatory variables in 1.6. This tests for the potential differential impact of NWI and NPI on PRSA, i.e. the one not captured already in the coefficient of ΔNPDI. A positive coefficient of NWI and/or NPI in this framework would indicate that non-controlling households save out of the level of their NWI and NPI, as well as saving out of their changing incomes. The above test is performed in 2.1 in Table 2. It can be seen that the coefficients of both NWI and NPI are insignificantly different from zero, lending support to our previous findings and thus the Galbraith–Marglin hypothesis.

Equations 2.2, 2.3 and 2.4 in Table 2 test the 'Kaldorian' hypothesis (2.2 and 2.4) and its related 'Managerialist' Saving Function (2.2 and 2.3). Equation 2.2 obtains from 1.6 by relaxing in the latter the (already found to be valid) restrictions that the coefficients of NPDI and lagged NPDI are equal, and similarly that the coefficients of NWI and NPI are equal, and then imposing on it the (already found to be invalid) restriction that the coefficients of NWI and NILP are equal.

The latter is the conventional wisdom as reflected in the official statistics and the studies on differential 'propensities' examined so far.[15] It turns out from 2.2 that the coefficients of NWI and NPI are very close to each other, in line with previous studies, which focussed on personal sector disposable shares only. An equality restriction on the coefficients of NWI and NPI gives rise to 2.3, a test of the 'M'SF. The restriction is accepted at the 5% level of an F-test.

As they stand, 2.2 and 2.3 appear to lend support to the 'Kaldorian' hypothesis and the 'M'SF in that the coefficient of CORE in both appears to be significantly higher than the coefficients of WI and NPI. The above can be tested by restricting the coefficients of NPI and CORE to be equal. This gives rise to 2.4, which directly tests the 'Kaldorian' hypothesis (1). The restriction is rejected at the 5% level of an F-test.

It would appear from 2.2, 2.3 and 2.4 that the aggregate proportions of

Table 2. Tests of the Galbraith–Marglin hypothesis, the 'Kaldorian' hypothesis and the 'Managerialist' Saving Function

Annual UK data: 1952–84. Dependent variable PRSA

Eqn No.	Constant	$\Delta NPDI_t$	NWI_t	NPI_t	WI_t	PI_t	$PSDI_t$	$CORE_t$	$COSA_t$	$NPDI_{t-1}$	NPS_{t-1}	$\bar{R}^2$	SSE	$\hat{\rho}$
2.1	−3847.64	0.19*	0.04	0.02				1.04*			0.64*	0.9911	425×10^{11}	−0.19
	(−1.43)	(2.10)	(0.90)	(0.34)				(15.10)			(3.10)			(−1.03)
2.2	−3170.74			0.39*	0.37*		1.14*			−0.33*	0.98*	0.9956	390×10^{11}	−0.35†
	(−1.50)			(6.45)	(5.72)		(19.66)			(−4.09)	(5.37)			(−1.95)
2.3	−3337.54†					0.39*	1.13*			−0.35*	1.04*	0.9959	405×10^{11}	−0.39*
	(−1.64)					(6.57)	(20.43)			(−4.54)	(6.09)			(−2.22)
2.4	−1528.89*				0.36*	0.52*				−0.09	−0.06	0.8198	722×10^{11}	0.81*
	(−2.16)				(5.44)	(6.24)				(−1.04)	(−0.23)			(7.23)

't' ratios in parentheses.

Δ denotes the first difference.

* denotes significance at the 5% level.

† denotes significance at the 10% level.

71

personal and private sector income shares saved are positive and significantly different from zero. In particular, the proportion of aggregate wage income would appear to be 0.36 while that of aggregate profits, 0.52. Still, the interpretation of these findings is not straightforward. In our framework, the coefficients of all WI, PI and PSDI do not represent real propensities to save of the non-controlling households. Rather they represent an amalgam of transient saving out of households changing incomes, real propensities (already found here to be equal to zero) and contractual saving that corporate leaders save on behalf of the non-controlling households within the corporate sector. In this sense the term propensity is misleading in that it conveys the idea that non-controlling households act according to their psychological urges, or alternatively that they are 'sovereign'.

Quite apart from issues of interpretation, the very statistical validity of equations 2.2, 2.3 and 2.4 is highly questionable. In our framework, the above equations have been obtained by imposing invalid restrictions on our preferred equations 1.3 and 1.4 and the equivalent of 1.3, equation 1.6. All equations 2.2, 2.3 and 2.4 are subject to first-order autocorrelation, 2.2 at the 10% level and 2.3 and 2.4 at the 5% level, which can be viewed as a sign of misspecification potentially arising from the very imposition of these invalid restrictions.

To conclude, our results lend support to the CCSF, i.e. the idea that NILP and CORE are saved in higher proportions than non-controlling shareholders' disposable income shares, and thus have a positive impact on financial capital accumulation. Moreover, we found support for the Galbraith–Marglin hypothesis according to which households (in our framework only the non-controlling ones) do not save out of the level of their incomes, but only when their incomes are changing. The 'Kaldorian' hypothesis and the 'Managerialist' Saving Function can be obtained from the CCSF by imposing on it invalid restrictions. This casts doubt not only on the term 'propensity' but also on the very statistical validity of the obtained results. Our support for the CCSF also casts severe doubt on the implications of the LCH according to which the proportions of NILP and CORE saved should be equal to those of NWI and NPI.

Starting from 1.6, assuming that COSA are affected by their one period lagged value, including the latter as an additional explanatory variable in 1.6 and restricting its coefficient to be equal to that of lagged NPS, gave the following equation:

$$PRSA_t = 2979.82^* + 0.23^* \, \Delta NPDI_t + 0.80^* \, COSA_t$$
$$(-7.55) \quad (4.82) \quad\quad\quad (16.38)$$

$$+ 0.40^* \, PRSA_{t-1} + 0.04 v_{t-1} + u_t \quad\quad\quad (7)$$
$$(10.74) \quad\quad\quad (0.23)$$

$$\bar{R}^2 = 0.9964 \quad SSE = 186 \times 10^{11} \quad LM = 6.07.$$

The above restriction was accepted at the 5% level of an F-test. Equation (7) can thus be seen as an early (and incomplete) attempt to estimate a private saving function incorporating the determinants of both NPS and COSA, see also Furstenberg (1981). It can also result from the LCH, i.e. (A) defined in terms of PRSA and PRI. An unrestricted version of the latter would be an equation as (7) but which also includes lagged COSA as an explanatory variable. Setting this last variable equal to zero would give (7) a restriction which we tested and found to be accepted at the 5% level of an F-test. Equation (7) obviously casts doubt on the LCH, according to which the coefficients of COSA and lagged COSA should be equal to each other and both equal to the coefficient of ΔNPDI. Instead the coefficient of COSA is significantly higher than that of ΔNPDI, as an F-test indicated. Equation (7) does not suffer from AR 1 and/or higher-order autocorrelation and/or misspecification as indicated by the LM. Testing all hypotheses summarized in Table 2 in its framework gave support to our previous findings.

These hypotheses were finally tested in the framework of an extended LCH *à la* Feldstein (1978). Namely, accepting the (already found to be invalid) restrictions of the LCH, we defined (A) in terms of PRSA and PRI. We then included CORE and NILP as additional explanatory variables in the regression to test for their potential differential impact on PRSA, i.e. the one not already captured in the coefficient of PRI. In this framework perfect substitution is implied by a coefficient of NILP and/or CORE equal to zero. A positive and significant coefficient would imply imperfect substitution and/or independence, depending on its value. In the resulting equation the coefficients of CORE and NILP were found to be positive, significant and very close to each other. An F-test accepted the restriction that they were equal, giving rise to the equation:

$$PRSA_t = -2392.41^* + 0.23^* \Delta PRI_t + 0.61^* COSA_t$$
$$\quad\quad (-5.73) \quad\quad (4.47) \quad\quad\quad (7.59)$$

$$+ 0.54^* PRSA_{t-1} - 0.02v_{t-1} + u_t \quad\quad (8)$$
$$\quad (8.82) \quad\quad\quad\quad (-0.13)$$

$$\bar{R}^2 = 0.9962 \quad SSE = 198 \times 10^{11} \quad LM = 8.97.$$

It follows from (8) that the implications of the LCH are rejected in its very own framework. Equation (8) performs satisfactorily although it is inferior to (7) in terms of all $\bar{R}^2$, SSE and LM. This is not surprising given our previous findings that (8) incorporates a number of invalid restrictions. The hypotheses of Table 2 were also tested in the framework of (8). The results are not reported (to economize space) but are available from the author on request. Suffice it to note here that they give support to our previous findings.

The validity of our conclusions above depends of course on the reliability, or otherwise, of our results. Regarding the usual statistical problems in frameworks such as ours, none of our preferred equations 1.3, 1.4, 1.6 and (7) appear to suffer from multicollinearity, judging at least from the low standard errors. First-order autocorrelation was not present in any of these equations either. Similarly no evidence of higher (up to fourth-) order autocorrelation and misspecification was found in our preferred equations 1.4 and (7). Regarding finally the potential problem of Simultaneous Equations Bias (SEB), our theoretical analysis would lend support to the idea that NILP and CORE are not determined by NPS. If this is accepted then our equations become part of a recursive system which can be estimated with OLS and without the SEB problem.

Perhaps more important to the above discussion of statistical problems is the fact that our results happen to lend support to the theoretical analysis of this and the previous chapter. This 'coincidence' in itself would suggest that our results are of some value. Still, given the nature of our data and the state of the art, no claim of conclusiveness is made here.[16] The best interpretation one should put to our results is probably that they do not reject our theoretical analysis so far, which is encouraging.

Appendix

The similarities and differences of the estimated forms of alternative consumption/saving hypotheses have long aroused interest. An important result along these lines is Swamy (1968), who demonstrated the equivalence between the LCH and the H–T model in the form of the equation:

$$S_t = d_1 \Delta Y_t + d_2 S_{t-1}. \tag{A}$$

This result was acknowledged by both Houthakker and Taylor (1970) and Modigliani (1975). Another well-established result in the literature is that the estimated form of the AE/PI and the SL/HP hypotheses of consumption are associated with the existence of a lagged consumption variable in the right-hand side of these equations, see e.g. Wallis (1979). What has not been established so far, at least as far as we know, is that the latter type of consumption equations can also be brought in the form of (A). Further, that the recently popular 'error correction' model can also be brought in this form. The aim of this Appendix is to demonstrate the above, by focussing on the deterministic parts of the estimated forms of the hypotheses concerned. In so doing we first rederive the Swamy result in a way different from Swamy's.

Consider first the Houthakker–Taylor (1970) model. It starts from the proposition that desired wealth, W^*, is a function of income, Y; i.e.

$$W_t^* = f Y_t. \tag{A.1}$$

Assuming that saving is proportional to the difference between W^* and actual wealth, W

$$S_t = s(W_t^* - W_{t-1}) \tag{A.2}$$

differencing (A.2) and substituting (A.1) for W^*, they obtained (A).

Modigliani (1975), on the other hand, writes the LCH as

$$C_t = \alpha Y_t + (\delta - r) W_t \tag{A.3}$$

75

where r is the rate of return on assets and α and δ are constants. From the definition of wealth,

$$W_t = W_{t-1} + Y_{t-1} - C_{t-1} \tag{A.4}$$

it follows that,

$$C_t = \alpha Y_t + (\delta - r - \alpha)Y_{t-1} + (1 - \delta + r)C_{t-1}. \tag{A.5}$$

Substituting in (A.5) C_t for its equivalent $Y_t - S_t$ gives rise once more to (A) where $d_1 = (1-\alpha)$ and $d_2 = (1+r-\delta)$.

(A) can also be derived from the PA model of consumption if we equate the desired or equilibrium value of consumption C^* to income, i.e. assume a propensity to save equal to zero. Formally, if

$$C_t^* = Y_t, \tag{A.6}$$

then from

$$\Delta C_t = \zeta(Y_t - C_{t-1}), \tag{A.7}$$

solving for C_t and substituting the latter for its equivalent $Y_t - S_t$, gives (A) where now $d_1 = d_2 = (1-\zeta)$.

The SL/HP and AE/PI models can be written as:

$$C_t = \xi_1 Y + \xi_2 C_{t-1}, \tag{A.8}$$

see e.g. Wallis (1979), Davis (1984). Substituting C for $Y - S$ gives,

$$S_t = (1-\xi_1)Y_t - \xi_1 Y_{t-1} + \xi_2 S_{t-1}. \tag{A.9}$$

This is equivalent to (A) for $(1-\xi_1) = \xi_1$, i.e. for $\xi = 0.5$; which can be tested on estimation.

Finally the 'error correction' model of Marglin (1975) is given in discrete time form in Davidson *et al.* (1975) and Hendry (1983) as:

$$\Delta C_t = \theta_1 \Delta Y_t + \theta_2 S_{t-1}. \tag{A.10}$$

Substituting ΔC_t for $C_t - C_{t-1}$ and ΔY_t for $Y_t - Y_{t-1}$, and solving for S_t, gives once more (A) where now

$$d_1 = (1-\theta_1) \quad \text{and} \quad d_2 = (1-\theta_2).$$

The above establish our proposition that the estimated forms of the deterministic parts of all the above hypotheses are consistent with (A) and that in this sense the latter becomes *ceteris paribus* a 'general' estimated equation for the examination of saving behaviour.

CHAPTER 5

Capital accumulation and the realization of profits

At the aggregate level the tendency towards SOMP will tend to result in an increasingly higher proportion of private disposable income being controlled by the corporate sector; a direct product of the appearance and growth of (direct and indirect) shareholding. *Ceteris paribus* this will tend to result in an increasingly higher proportion of private disposable income being retained within the corporate sector, in the form of corporate retained earnings and/or the net inflow to life and pension funds. With less than perfect substitutability between personal and corporate saving, the above will tend to reduce the share of consumers' expenditure to private disposable income. In this sense the tendency towards SOMP will tend to introduce an underconsumptionist tendency in advanced capitalist economies, a situation where consumers' expenditure is insufficient to buy the full capacity (consumption goods) product of the corporate sector.

An underconsumptionist tendency contains the seeds of a realization failure, a situation where the total effective demand of the private sector, consumption plus investment, is insufficient to absorb the full capacity (consumption and production goods) product of the corporate sector, thus failing to realize the potential profits of firms. The above need not be the case if private investment increases sufficiently to compensate for the tendency of consumption to decline. Assuming that capitalist firms produce for profits rather than consumption, the latter is a possibility, necessitating the analysis of the determinants of private investment.

It is widely believed that the rate of profit to total capital stock is the main determinant of investment as it is taken to determine the future profit expectations of the capitalists. The profit rate can be decomposed into three constituent parts; the share of profits, the rate of capacity utilization and the ratio of capacity to capital. Focussing on disposable income shares, the tendency towards SOMP will tend to increase the share of profits, exerting a positive impact on the profit rate and thus investment. However, the tendency of consumption to decline may induce firms to restrict output, rather than reduce prices, which will tend to increase excess capacity in the consumption goods industries. If this is the case – and assuming a constant capacity to capital ratio – the effects of underconsumption on capacity utilization will tend to put definite limits on potential increases in profit rates and investment, making a realization crisis distinctly possible.

The tendency towards realization crisis will tend to be exacerbated if the third constituent part of the rate of profits, the productivity of capital, declines; due e.g. to increases in the organic composition of capital – the ratio of constant to variable capital (labour). In this sense our analysis is consistent with the Marxist theory of the 'law' of the declining rate of profits, a result of a rising tendency in the organic composition of capital, due to labour saving technological change.

In the above scenario the tendency towards underconsumption is inherent in advanced capitalist countries to the same extent that the appearance of the joint stock company and its associated tendency towards SOMP are; provided of course that no full substitutability exists between personal and corporate saving. In this sense our suggestions are in stark contrast to the neoclassical theory, according to which no secular decline in the consumption to private disposable income ratio can occur against households' will. Our suggestions can accommodate, however, existing Keynesian and Marxist views on underconsumption. According to the former it is the presumption of the existence of differential saving propensities between profit income (earners) on the one hand and wage income (earners) on the other, along with potential shifts in the distribution of income between these two classes that may lead to an underconsumptionist tendency. In the most widely accepted version of the Marxist theory the ability of the giant firms to increase their profit margins over time by decreasing their marginal (wage and material) costs leads to a tendency towards a rising 'surplus' (total corporate profits plus the wasteful expenditures of firms and the state). This makes consumption and investment decline as a proportion of the 'surplus', over time, while it tends to increase the wasteful expenditure of firms and the state, so that the increasing 'surplus' is absorbed.

Although our analysis can be cast in terms of the Keynesian focus on differential saving propensities between wage and profit income, we suggest that it is more general than the Keynesian view. It accounts for the role of pension funds and provides an explanation as to why shifts in the after-tax functional distribution of income occur. Similarly it is more general than, and complementary to, the Marxist view in that it does not require the conscious attempts of firms to increase profit margins for an underconsumptionist tendency to operate. In our framework, I suggest, increases in the inequality of income distribution and the associated tendency of the 'surplus' to rise, are not necessarily the result of the actions of individual firms, albeit such actions would strengthen the above tendencies.

A realization crisis arising through reductions in personal consumer expenditure not fully offset by increases in private domestic investment will tend to give rise to a tendency towards an increasing ratio of 'excess saving' (the part of private disposable income neither consumed nor invested) to private disposable income. The coexistence of 'excess saving' for investment, and deficient demand at the domestic level with its associated pressures on profitability, may tend to induce firms to look for overseas markets, to export and/or undertake direct foreign activities. In this sense we can see the internationalization of production and the appearance of the transnational corporation to be in a historical sense the inevitable result of the capital accumulation process and its associated effects on demand and profitability at the domestic levels of advanced capitalist economies.

The existence of a tendency towards SOMP, despite its adverse long-run effects on effective demand, can be seen as the result of the decentralized nature of market economies, i.e. the 'anarchy' of the capitalist system. Firms are doing what they consider to be good for themselves and this is not necessarily good for the system as a whole. In a closed economy the SOMP process is sooner or later going to come to a standstill, as reductions in effective demand defeat the very need for further finance for expansion. With internationalized production, however, the SOMP process may continue for as long as profitable investment outlets exist abroad and potential saving is available at the domestic level. In this sense the internationalization of production may tend to prolong a realization crisis. The degree and nature of international activities of a country's capital, on the other hand, may be a factor explaining the degree of the relative performance of capitalist countries.

A realization crisis is inherent in advanced capitalist countries, but only as a tendency. A number of counterforces may hinder the realization of the tendency as a real crisis. Most notable are the advertising and technological change policies of firms, and various activities of states. We suggest, however, that the effects of such policies are not unambiguous or unidirectional. Their role lies mainly in their ability to delay the appearance of a recession rather than in being able to ensure a sustained expansion.

The available historical statistics for the US and the UK appear to be in line with the above scenario, providing an explanation of the *initiating force* of the recent prolonged recession of these countries, the 'second slump', and the 'relative decline' of the UK. Our analysis can also explain the recent crisis if its insights are combined with those of other analyses. In particular it complements the post-Keynesian account of the 'cumulative decline' of the UK, and it is also consistent with the Marxist concerns with the rising militancy of labour, the role of the international 'orientation' of fractions of British capital and the role of the transnational corporations (TNCs) in contributing to the crisis. It sees all the latter, however, as the result rather than the initiating causes of the crisis. Still, results that once in existence can obtain their own momentum and become independent factors prolonging the recession.

The ability of international capital to find outlets for its products overseas suggests that the recent crisis may not be a crisis for capital as a whole, but rather a crisis for the vast majority of people who suffer the effects of deindustrialization and unemployment. The internationalization of the process towards SOMP, moreover, may set in motion forces leading to a global realization failure and stagnation. The ability of nation states to stop or reverse such tendencies may become increasingly slimmer due to the increasing bargaining power of transnational capital, which results from its ability to shift its operations to other countries at short notice.

The socialization of the ownership of the means of production and the realization of profits

The tendency towards SOMP through direct and indirect shareholding will tend to increase the share of corporate income (profits) to private disposable income. The reason for that is simple. Starting from a situation where corporate income is, let us say, x per cent of private disposable income, then, as some households are tempted (or forced) to buy corporate shares, the share of corporate to private income will tend to become higher than x, *ceteris paribus*.[1] Assuming that the pay-out ratio is constant, the above tendency of the share of profits to increase will imply a tendency in the shares of both retained earnings and dividends to disposable private income to increase. If firms consciously attempt to reduce the long-run pay-out rate or adjust dividends sluggishly to their long-run ratio in the face of increasing profits, an increasing share of profits can be consistent with a constant and/or declining share of dividends to private disposable income.

It follows from the above that, unless firms strive or are forced to increase the long-run pay-out rate, the tendency towards SOMP and its associated tendency of the share of profits to increase will tend to result in an increasingly higher proportion of private disposable income taking the form of corporate retained earnings, i.e. an increasingly lower proportion being available for consumption. Provided that households are not able to fully offset the increase in the share of retentions to private disposable income the latter will tend to result in a secular decline of the share of consumers' expenditure to private disposable income. In the above sense the tendency towards SOMP introduces an underconsumptionist tendency in advanced capitalist economies, i.e. a situation where the ability of the consumers to buy the full capacity consumption goods output of the corporate sector is being undermined.

In the perfectly competitive world of orthodox microeconomics textbooks firms producing consumption goods and faced with reduced demand for their products will respond by reducing prices. In today's oligopolistic market structures, however arguably characterized by non-price rather than price competition, see Koutsoyiannis (1982), it is unlikely that in the face of declining demand firms will respond (only) by reducing prices. It is more likely that, partly due to fear of retaliation by rivals leading to a price war, firms will react to a decline in consumption by restricting their output, while perhaps at the same time spending more on research and development, advertising and other selling expenses so as to compete with their rivals.[2]

Even if it is assumed that firms' response to declining consumption would be to partly reduce prices and partly restrict output, the end result would be some restriction in output, and thus an associated decline in the capacity utilization of the capital of these firms. This would lead to a decline in their demand for the product of firms producing capital goods, which in its turn would lead to an increase in the latters' excess capacity. It follows that overall it is likely that an initial decline in consumers' expenditure may result in lower output levels and an increase in excess capacity in the economy at large.

It we limit our analysis at the moment to a closed economy with no state sector, it is possible that restrictions in output and capacity utilization arising via reductions in consumers' expenditure, will have further effects on private investment and output. It is conceivable, to start with, that the demand of firms for investment is a derived one, i.e. it is *directly* linked to changes in consumption. The idea is implicit in the simple 'accelerator principle' which views investment as a function of the change in output, see Sherman (1979). Alternatively, it is possible that consumption affects investment *indirectly* via its effects on output and capacity utilization. Namely, reductions in consumption lead to a decline in output and capacity utilization, see Steindl (1952), Rowthorn (1981), which in their turn lead to a reduction in investment.[3] In both the above cases, the end product of a decline in consumption would be expected to be a decline in private investment as well.

It is widely accepted that perhaps the single most important determinant of a firm's investment is its rate of profit, see Sherman (1979), Rowthorn

(1981), Sawyer (1982), as this is thought to determine the capitalists' future profit expectations, see Weisskopf (1979). Following the last mentioned author, we can write the profit rate of the private sector (in price terms) as:

$$\Pi/K = (\Pi/Y)(Y/Z)(Z/K) \tag{1}$$

where K is the capital stock of the private sector, Z is its full capacity output, and Π and Y are private sector's profits and income respectively. The first term of equation (1) thus denotes the share of profits or, in Marxist terminology, the rate of exploitation of labour. The second is the rate of capacity utilization, and the third, the capacity to capital ratio or alternatively the productivity of capital, see Sherman (1979). Our analysis, so far, would suggest that the tendency towards SOMP will tend to increase the first term in (1), but reduce the second. It has no immediate implication on the third. Overall, the impact of SOMP on the profit rate would appear to depend on the relative strength of the two opposing factors.

The implication of the above is that, unless dramatic changes take place in the profit share, the SOMP-induced underconsumptionist tendency puts definite limits on potential increases in the rate of profit and thus private investment. Coupled with our analysis of the potential direct and indirect effects of changes in consumption on investment, the above imply that it is highly unlikely that, following a reduction in consumption, private investment will increase sufficiently so as to fully compensate for the reductions in consumption. It would appear more likely that private investment will not increase by as much as the decline in consumption, will remain constant, or even fall.

In all the above cases the result will be a tendency towards a realization crisis, a situation where the total effective demand of the private sector is insufficient to buy the full capacity product of this sector, so that firms cannot sell their products at a profitable price, thus failing to realize their potential profits. The crisis will tend to be reflected partly in terms of increasing excess capacity and partly in terms of a tendency towards increasing 'excess saving', i.e. the part of private income neither invested nor consumed.

To summarize the argument so far, capitalists strive to accumulate profits; this results in a tendency towards SOMP, thus, *ceteris paribus*, to an increasing proportion of private income not being available to households for consumption. This tends to result in a secular decline of the ratio of consumption to private income. The latter in its turn tends to affect private investment adversely, either directly or indirectly, via its effects on output and capacity utilization. Reductions in capacity utilization, on the other hand, tend to put limits on the potential increase in the profit rate that arises through the effects of SOMP on the share of profits. The end product is a tendency towards a realization failure, which manifests itself as a tendency for excess capacity and excess saving to increase.

The above scenario has been couched in terms of the tendency towards SOMP as well as differential saving 'propensities' between corporate and personal saving – or alternatively the lack of perfect substitutability between the two. In this sense our approach is in stark contrast to the neoclassical theory according to which a secular decline in the share of consumption to private income could only be consistent with changes in factors affecting the preferences of consumers. It can accommodate, however, the Keynesian view. According to that, an underconsumptionist tendency can arise if the distribution of income is changed in favour of profits, given the presumed existence of a higher 'propensity' to save profit income rather than wage income, see Bleaney (1976).[4] As explained in the last two chapters, the growth of occupational pension funds suggests that the Keynesian focus on a higher propensity to save profits fails to account for the role of pension funds. The Keynesian argument can become consistent with our approach here if it is rephrased in terms of corporate and personal sector saving propensities, as in Kregel (1971). Even so, however, the Keynesian approach lacks generality in that it provides no reason as to why changes in the distribution of income should secularly, if at all, take place. Such an explanation is provided in the Marxist approach to the theory of underconsumption, in particular that of Baran and Sweezy (1967) and Cowling (1982).

Baran and Sweezy (1967) based their analysis upon the earlier tradition of Kalecki (see e.g. the collection of some of his writing in Kalecki, 1971), Sweezy (1942), Steindl (1952) and Baran (1962). The above contributions are by now widely known and discussed, see e.g. Bleaney's (1976) survey, so they will not be given further consideration here. The starting point of Baran and Sweezy was to take the 'giant firm' as their unit of analysis. They suggested that the primary consideration of such firms, which dominate today's advanced capitalist countries, is to attempt to cut overtime, their marginal costs, i.e. their wages, and material costs, relative to the price they charge. Put another way, giant firms are said to be powerful enough to be able to pass on any increases on their wage and/or material costs bill to the consumers by increasing their prices. When, however, costs are declining, firms do not reduce their prices, basically due to their fear of the potentially damaging effects on their profits of a price war initiated as rival firms follow suit in order to retain their market share. The end product of such behaviour is a tendency of the profit margins of giant firms to rise.

Aggregating over the whole economy, the tendency towards increasing profit margins will tend to result in a tendency towards an increasing 'surplus'; the sum of aggregate profits (corporate profits, rent, interest and income from self-employment) as well as the wasteful expenditures of firms and the state, e.g. on advertising and military expenditures. However, the tendency of the potential surplus to increase may not be realized as profits. With increasing profit margins, Baran and Sweezy suggest, the (often conscious) attempts by firms to be sluggish in adjusting dividends to their (in the long run constant) pay-out rate will result in a higher proportion of income being retained and a lower proportion being distributed. Thus consumption will tend to be an increasingly lower proportion of the 'surplus'. The case of investment is similar, as it pays giant firms to suppress inventions for as long as old plants are still profitable. Wasteful expenditures in advertising and military spending accordingly tend to become an increasingly higher proportion of the surplus. In the absence of the latter, but also of a number of 'epoch-making' innovations such as the railways, capitalism would, according to Baran and Sweezy, have been led to a profound recession.

Cowling (1982) provides a formal synthesis and extension of ideas in the Kalecki, Steindl, and Baran and Sweezy tradition, also referred to as the 'Monopoly Capital' tradition, see Fine and Murfin (1984). A crucial notion in Cowling is that of 'excess capacity' as a barrier to entry; an idea first developed by Steindl (1952) and more recently popularized by Spence (1977). The existence of excess capacity (intentional or unintentional) is said to provide an irreversible and therefore credible threat to potential entrants that output will be increased after entry, thus prices will be reduced, making it unprofitable for them to enter. This implies a separability of the price-output decision of firms and the decision on what to do about entry in that firms may pursue policies of unconstrained short-run profit maximization; see Sawyer (1982a).[5]

Under the above assumption Cowling is able to formalize the Kaleckian notion of the 'degree of monopoly' (more conventionally the price–cost margin, i.e. the ratio of the variation of the price from marginal cost, divided by the price), in terms of market structure and conduct variables, namely the elasticity of demand, the degree of concentration and the degree of collusion in an industry. Aggregating first for the industry and then the economy as a whole, it is shown that, under the assumptions of constant marginal costs and vertically integrated domestic industries, the degree of monopoly determines the share of gross capitalist profits (inclusive of salaries) to Gross National Income. The tendency towards monopolization of markets will tend to increase the degree of monopoly for the economy as a whole as giant firms increase their prices and restrict their output. Baran and Sweezy's notion of the 'surplus' can thus be seen in this framework in terms of an increasing 'degree of monopoly'. Increases in the degree of monopoly will result in a decline in the share of workers' income (and thus consumption) to Gross National Income. The underlying tendency towards a realization crisis may tend to be mitigated by a number of factors, such as capitalist consumption, advertising, managerial consumption, export surplus and increasing intervention by the state. The effects of such factors, however, are not automatic and are said to contain the seeds of a possibly deeper crisis.

Our analysis has been couched in terms of increases in corporate saving shares due to SOMP, leading to an increasing share of profits rather than in terms of increases in the degree of monopoly leading to the same result. In doing so our approach makes explicit the importance of controlled, rather than owned income, particularly the role of pension funds. By simply focussing on the share of profits, an increase in pension funds would imply a reduction in the profits share and thus an increase in consumption, especially under the assumption that all wage income is consumed, Marx (1959), Ricardo (1973), Kalecki (1971), Rowthorn (1981).[6] Following from the above, in our framework an underconsumptionist tendency can exist even in the absence of increases in the 'degree of monopoly' and the share of profits. This may be the case, for example, if, in a recession, bankruptcies, etc., result in actual profits declining at a rate sufficient to offset the effects of SOMP on the share of profits. In this case the tendency towards underconsumption may still operate for as long as the rate of decline of dividends is higher than that of retentions. It is only if the rate of decline of retentions is higher than that of the rate of decline of dividends that the tendency towards underconsumption should be expected to reverse, *ceteris paribus*.

Given the above, our analysis could be viewed as alternative and complementary to that of the 'Monopoly Capital' tradition. A potential additional difference is that our focus is not on the policies of individual firms but rather on the very logic of the process of capital accumulation.[7] Underconsumptionist tendencies and realization failures are here seen as the result of interruptions in this process, see Wolff (1978), resulting from the associated tendency towards SOMP, rather than the policies pursued by individual firms. Such policies will tend to strengthen the tendency towards crisis, which, however, can operate even in their absence.

The tendency towards a realization crisis will tend to be exacerbated if, for example, labour-saving technological change results in a tendency of the third term in equation (1) to fall. Marx (1959) formulated his 'law of the declining rate of profit' exactly in terms of capitalism's progressive nature tending to result in an increase in the organic composition of capital – the constant capital (machinery) to the variable capital (labour) ratio – due to labour-saving technological progress. Importantly our analysis indicates in a common framework that Marx's theories of underconsumption and the 'law of declining rate of profits' are not irreconcilable.[8] Rather, they may neatly work simultaneously. The capitalists' motivation to accumulate, for example, can be seen as the underlying force that leads to the tendency towards SOMP with its associated effects on the share of profits and capacity utilization while at the same time leading to a rise in the organic composition and thus a fall in the productivity of capital and the rate of profit. As the latter is consistent with a tendency for a rising 'degree of monopoly' and the share of profits, the above scenario shows the compatibility between the 'orthodox' Marxist tradition, e.g. Mandel (1975), and the 'Monopoly Capital' tradition of the theory of capitalist crisis.

It has already been pointed out that in an oligopolistic market structure firms may compete in ways other than price competition, such as advertising and research and development (R & D). It could be suggested that such forms of expenditure might mitigate a tendency towards realization crisis. The case of advertising, for example, is very interesting. First, advertising expenditure constitutes a form of investment, and thus adds directly to effective demand, see e.g. Rothschild (1942). It is widely held, moreover, that advertising messages induce a higher consumption expenditure, further adding to effective demand, see Galbraith (1967), Baran and Sweezy (1967), Cowling (1982). The problem with this latter effect, in our framework, is that the tendency towards SOMP implies an increasingly lower proportion of private income being available for consumption anyway. This may tend to make this particular effect of advertising potential rather than real.

It is also widely held in the industrial organization literature that advertising, acting as a barrier to entry, see e.g. Hay and Morris (1979) for a survey, has positive effects on the profitability of established firms. There is substantial evidence to support this argument, see Koutsoyiannis (1982) for a survey. Although increased profits will tend to increase the share of profit, and thus induce higher investment, they will also tend to reduce the share of wages and thus reduce consumption, capacity utilization, output and therefore investment. Finally, advertising is undertaken not only by manufacturing firms trying to induce consumption but also by financial institutions trying to attract saving. This latter effect may also partly offset the alleged effects of advertising on consumption. It follows that the overall effect of advertising on effective demand is not easy to predict on *a priori* grounds. That such an effect will be positive is by no means a foregone conclusion.

The case of research and development (R & D) is not very dissimilar to that of advertising. Expenditure on R & D adds directly on effective demand. At the same time, however, R & D may serve as a deterrent to potential entrants, thus leading to higher prices and restrictions in output. To the extent that new inventions are not suppressed, see Baran and Sweezy (1967), technological changes may lead to increases in investment, see Rowthorn (1981). At the same time, however, they may tend to increase the share of profits, particularly if they are of the labour-saving nature. Stoneman (1984) has evidence that technological change increases investment but at the same time it tends to redistribute income to profits. Once more the overall effect of R & D on effective demand is not certain to be unidirectional.

It can be concluded from the above that, in a closed economy with no state sector, a SOMP-induced underconsumptionist tendency incorporates the seeds of a realization crisis. A number of factors may tend to mitigate this crisis, but their effects are not unidirectional.

Realization crisis, internationalization of production and the role of the state

In a closed economy, the continuation of the tendency towards SOMP despite its adverse effects on effective demand can be seen as the result of the 'anarchy' of the capitalist mode of production. In decentralized market economies, firms' behaviour is motivated by what they consider to be good for themselves, without regard for, or knowledge of, the aggregate implications of their actions. Obtaining finance from the public in particular helps firms to grow without industrial capitalists risking their losing control to financial capitalists, banks, etc. In the aggregate, however, such actions set in operation forces which tend to defeat the very need for expansion and thus SOMP. It follows that in the closed economy the need for expansion and SOMP will eventually tend to come to a standstill.[9] In the above sense it is the tendency towards SOMP domestically which tends to lead to realization failures at home.

The tendency towards SOMP and its associated effects on consumption, capacity utilization and profitability pressures would tend to result in firms finding themselves with insufficient domestic demand to absorb their products, as well as an excess capacity in saving. This coexistence may tend to induce firms to look for overseas markets to export their products and/or undertake directly production activities abroad. Thus, starting from a closed economy, one can see, in a historical sense, the internationalization of production and the appearance of the transnational corporation as the combined result of the impact of SOMP on effective demand and 'excess saving'.[10] In this sense, it is the tendency towards the crisis that leads to internationalization of production and not vice versa.

The possibility of firms exporting their products and/or of investing overseas has obvious important implications for our analysis. Exports provide domestic firms with a source of effective demand for their products, thus allowing them to carry on investing domestically despite any underconsumptionist tendencies. This will tend to offset a realization crisis in two ways. First, through increasing private domestic investment and second via increasing export surpluses. It will also allow firms to carry on the process of SOMP domestically despite its associated effects on consumption. The case of foreign investment is more complicated. Portfolio investment, first, will tend to provide capitalists with an outlet for their 'excess saving'. This export of financial capital may tend to increase the domestic share of profits, but its effects on domestic investment are not straightforward. Capitalists may simply carry on their portfolio investment overseas, for as long as this is profitable. Foreign direct investment (FDI) will also provide firms with an outlet for their 'excess saving'. To the extent, however, that FDI does not concentrate on activities fully complementary to the domestic industry, e.g. raw materials exported to the domestic economy, FDI may affect domestic investment adversely.

It follows that both portfolio investment and FDI may not result in adding enough to domestic private investment to offset a realization crisis. In contrast, the availability of overseas markets would allow firms to carry on the process of SOMP domestically for as long as there exist profitable outlets overseas and potential saving domestically. Financial capital may thus be accumulated where it is available and for as long as it is available, and invested where it appears to be more profitable. This would tend to prolong a realization crisis.

It has been suggested that once international capital appears, it may tend to view the whole world as its stage of operations, see e.g. Cowling (1985). Investment may be undertaken where and when it is more profitable, the primary considerations being a lower cost of production achieved through the choice of places characterized by a combination of factors: low wage rates, transport and material costs, 'appropriate' infrastructure, political 'stability', a 'xenophilic' state, and a loyal labour force.[11] 'Nationalism' need not necessarily be an important determinant of capitalists' decisions, leading perhaps to the deindustrialization of countries not considered worth investing in. The degree of international orientation of a country's capital, the importance of exports relative to total overseas operations, the nature of foreign investments, and the degree of commitment of capital to the national interests of its home base, may all tend to become factors affecting the relative performance of capitalist countries. In any case the importance of internationalized production lies in the ability of international capital to 'export' their excess saving and prolong the process of SOMP and thus the tendency towards realization crisis. In this sense the internationalization of production results in the continuation of the crisis.

It is widely believed that the international orientation (the 'cosmopolitan nature') of British capital may be one explanation of the so-called 'relative decline of the UK', see Hobsbawm (1969), Rowthorn (1980), Aaronovitch and Smith (1981). According to Hobsbawm, the ability of British capital to operate in the unexploited areas of the large British empire, profiting in an 'easy and cheap' way, induced it to retreat from industry to trade and finance. Rather than facing potential competition, British capital was increasingly becoming a parasite, and accordingly Britain a parasitic economy.

In more recent years a different version of this thesis appeared, attempting to explain the 'relative decline', in terms of intercapitalist conflicts. According to this argument, the 'relative autonomy' of the financial capital (the 'City' of London), from industrial capital, for the production of 'surplus value', deprives industry of finance for expansion and thus retards the development of the UK economy, see Minns (1981a, 1982), Coackley and Harris (1982). Regarding in particular pension funds, Minns suggested financial institutions tended to invest them abroad rather than at home, especially after the abolition of exchange controls in 1979. The part of pension funds invested overseas increased dramatically from 5% in 1979 to 32% in 1982. (It subsequently fell to around 15% in 1985.) This overseas investment of pension funds, Minns argued, would induce a deflationary tendency in the UK economy, eventually leaving the very source of the funds, the workers, unemployed.

Minns' position was intended to be a critique to the proponents of the 'finance capital' thesis, i.e. the idea that industrial and financial capital are increasingly fused, the one tending to undertake the role of the other and vice versa, see Hilferding (1981), Aaronovitch (1961), Mandel (1975). In particular, financial capital, it was argued, need not rely on domestic industrial capital for the generation of 'surplus value', so it becomes independent from domestic production. Still, this position fails to consider the possibility that the whole of capital in a particular state may be independent of production at the home level, i.e. become international. Intercapitalist differences in this sense should not necessarily be viewed in terms of financial versus industrial capital but rather in terms of an internationally oriented versus nationally oriented finance capital. Minns' own analysis suggests that only a relatively small proportion of pension funds in the UK were managed in-house, i.e. by the firms which operated them, despite the fact that cost considerations were not of paramount importance for this decision. It appears difficult to imagine why industrial capital, if in need of finance, decided to hand the management and control of the pension funds over to the financial capitalists if they 'disagreed' with their policies. It would appear more plausible to suggest that big industrial capital also 'preferred' to invest funds overseas, especially if, as suggested, underconsumptionist tendencies were in operation at home.

Whether financial capital alone, or financial capital as a whole, are 'cosmopolitan', the end product may be the same; stagnation at the home level. In this sense our analysis appears to be in line with the Hobsbawm thesis, but with a difference. In our framework it is the tendency towards SOMP that leads to realization crisis, thus internationalization of production and to the prolonging of the crisis, and not the 'preferences', 'orientations' or 'cosmopolitan nature' of capitalists. Put another way, all the latter are seen as endogenous to the system, i.e. determined by the underlying effects of SOMP on domestic effective demand. The existence of the British Empire with its associated effects on the need of British capital to compete are certainly important factors explaining the 'relative decline', but do not fully account for the initiating force of the decline.

Similar considerations apply to the post-Keynesian account of the 'relative decline'. According to this, the decline in competitiveness of the UK industry resulted in a demand constraint and thus in depressed investment. This has retarded technical progress and rendered UK products unattractive in world markets, leading to a contraction in exports, output and employment, see Stafford (1983) for a detailed survey and critique of the thesis. As the last-mentioned author observed, the problem with the post-Keynesian thesis is that it fails to explain the original cause of a decline in the UK competitiveness and its associated constraint in effective demand. It helps explain a process of cumulative decline but not the source of this process.

It has been suggested that the post-Keynesian thesis can be rescued if combined with the 'increased militancy of labour' thesis, Stafford (1983). This latter thesis was originally advanced by Glyn and Sutcliffe (1972) to explain the relative decline of the UK, but a similar version has also been proposed by Botty and Crotty (1975) in order to explain the US crisis. A variation of the Glyn and Sutcliffe thesis was more recently advanced by Kilpatrick and Lawson (1980). In the Glyn and Sutcliffe version it is the combined impact of increasing international competition and increasing militancy of labour that resulted in the relative decline of the UK. The reason for the relatively stronger labour movement in the UK, on the other hand, is explained in Kilpatrick and Lawson in terms of its organization at a plant and company level, which prevented firms from increasing the degree of labour exploitation by increasing work intensity and/or by introducing new production techniques. This original source of decline in competitiveness is said to have eventually resulted, through a process of cumulative decline, in the relatively worse performance of the UK.

The problem with the combined post-Keynesian/increasing militancy of labour thesis appears to be its inability to explain the decline at a world level. It could be suggested, of course, that an increasing militancy of labour at a world level resulted in the recent crisis and the UK did worse because of its particularly strong working class. The problem in such a thesis, however, is that the relative decline in the competitiveness of one country should necessarily be associated with a relative increase in the competitiveness of some others. *Ceteris paribus*, this would increase the latters' ability to export and thus might affect positively private domestic investment. The end product might be a boost in effective demand and performance of such countries, and not a relatively smaller deterioration characterizing a period of crisis. It follows that, in the open economy, the increasing militancy of labour thesis appears to serve better the purposes of a theory of 'relative decline' than of a theory of crisis.

We have suggested so far that the tendency towards SOMP results in a tendency towards realization crisis, and this induces firms to undertake international activities. In this framework the (degree of) labour militancy and its nature have a very important role to play. To the extent that labour unions attempt to protect the real wage of those at work, resist labour-saving innovations and/or try to resist falls in the level of employment, the power of the labour movement would appear to contribute to the crisis. Firms' attempts to reduce costs and increase their competitiveness will tend to be frustrated and this may induce them to undertake international operations. A strong labour movement in this framework would be one that was able to constrain their domestic capital from pursuing a strategy of deindustrialization. In this sense it might be suggested that it was the *lack* of militancy by British workers that contributed further to the crisis and not vice versa, see Rowthorn (1980). Semantics apart, it may be concluded from the above that the militancy of labour thesis is not necessarily inconsistent with our approach here. The main difference lies in that we see it as a contributory factor to the relative decline of the UK, rather than the initiating force of the decline. Moreover, to the extent that the increasing militancy was an attempt to protect workers' interests in response to capitalists' attempts to relieve their pressures on profitability resulting from the tendency towards SOMP, increasing militancy may be seen as a result of, and a further contributory factor to, the crisis.

Missing in the above analysis is a discussion of the role of the capitalist state. There is a wide disagreement between authors in, for example, the neoclassical and Marxist tradition as to the exact aims and role of the state in capitalist societies, see e.g. Miliband (1973) and Jessop (1977) for surveys. Still it would appear to be the case that all versions of the above theories share in common the view that when faced with a tendency towards crisis, the state would attempt to mitigate it. If the above is accepted, then the question becomes, what is the best way for the state to intervene so that a crisis is mitigated? The main problem in this case is that a crisis manifests itself not through its causes but rather through its effects. What a capitalist state would observe is not the tendency towards SOMP but rather reductions in private effective demand and their associated pressures on profitability. It is plausible therefore to expect that the state would attempt to mitigate the crisis by attacking these effects.

Focussing, for example, on equation (1), the state might attempt to relieve capitalists' pressures on profitability by, for example, redirecting its expenditure from transfers to workers, to infrastructure for investment. Such policies would tend to increase the share and rate of profits, and thus affect private investment positively. At the same time, however, they would tend to reduce the wage and thus the consumption share, reinforcing the problems of realization. In a closed economy, this might speed up the manifestation of the crisis. In the open economy, it might induce firms to export and/or produce directly overseas. According to our previous analysis this might mitigate or prolong the crisis at the home level, depending on the nature of domestic capitalists' overseas operations.

An alternative course of state action could be to attempt to increase the wage and thus the consumption share by, for example, re-directing state expenditure to workers. In a closed economy, this would be expected to have a negative short-run effect on profit shares–rates and investment, but eventually the increased demand of consumers might result in increased investment and output. In the open economy, however, such policies might tend to render a particular state unattractive to domestic and/or overseas international capital. Faced with high wage rates, capitalists might once more choose to invest overseas.

The above assume no change in the budget. Such changes offer another lever of macro-economic management to the state. An increase in the budget deficit, for example, would increase effective demand, tending to mitigate a tendency towards realization crisis. Increased budget deficits, however, have to be financed by, for example, taxing workers and/or capitalists, and/or by external borrowing. In the latter case as debts and interest payments will eventually have to be repaid this might once more necessitate resorting to taxation. The latter, however, might tend to lead to inflationary pressures as capitalists attempt to shift the tax burden to workers by increasing prices, and workers resist by demanding higher wages. In a closed economy, some inflation (engineered or not) would appear to benefit profits and thus investment, see Rowthorn (1977). Still, it once more tends to accentuate the demand problems. More importantly, in the open economy, increased inflation eventually tends to undermine the competitiveness of the domestic economy, see Mandel (1975), thus contributing further to the crisis.[12]

It would appear from the above, that in the open economy no magic formula exists by which states can mitigate the tendency towards crisis, through demand management. What appears to be required here is a policy which will be aimed at attracting domestic and foreign capitalists to invest in a particular country and/or at preventing domestic capitalists from investing overseas. A restrictive policy of balanced budgets and in any case not increased deficits, combined with redirecting of expenditure to capital, may be such a policy. It might allow the profit share to increase, reduce inflation, increase competitiveness, and make the domestic economy an attractive place to invest for both domestic and foreign international capital. In the long run this may result in increased investment and employment, and thus consumption, and as a result lead to a virtuous circle of expansion.

A problem in the above policies lies with their implementation. In particular, reductions in the budget deficits are not easy, as a number of 'built-in' stabilizers, such as progressive tax structures and unemployment benefits, tend to increase state expenditure in the recession. The existence of such stabilizers implies that the success of such policies cannot be guaranteed unless the 'welfare state' is first dismantled. In this sense the expansionary fiscal policies of the post-war era could be viewed as 'policy mistakes', see Bleaney (1985), in that, by attempting to achieve full employment and by building-up the welfare state, they made any retreats to deflationary policies exceedingly difficult. This is more so given the certain political reaction to deflation by workers and their unions. Given that in our framework boom incorporates the seeds of, and eventually leads to, crisis, and assuming that deflation is viewed by the state as the solution to the latter, a certain level of unemployment becomes necessary even during the boom to facilitate a retreat to deflation when and if necessary.

Despite its apparent attractiveness, the long-run impact of deflation is not obvious. First the dismantling of the welfare state incorporates both a cost and a demand element. It reduces the cost to capital but increases the pressures on demand, by reducing consumption. Further, to the extent that its alleged benefits are realized by all states, the contribution of reduced inflation to international competitiveness may tend to become increasingly slimmer. Finally, adoption of deflationary policies at the international level might tend to facilitate a process towards a global realization failure.

More generally, the above possibility does exist. International capital might tend to pursue policies towards the SOMP in the places of its operations, facilitating and/or initiating a tendency towards realization crisis. The ability of TNCs to separate workers into country-specific groups moreover would tend to increase the bargaining power of such firms relative to workers, see Sugden (1985), and the capitalist states, see Radice (1975). The end product might tend to be a reduction of the wage share at a global level and an increasingly higher proportion of all private income being controlled by the corporate sector. If states attempt to accommodate rather than restrict the demands of international capital, this might tend to result in a global realization failure. The timing of the latter will depend crucially on the share of capitalist to the total world.

The above imply that crises may increasingly tend to become internationalized and thus prolonged. Still, from a purely economic point of view, there appears to be no obvious reason why this tendency towards global crises should lead to capitalism's demise. Although we do not here intend to develop a theory of the business cycle, it would appear plausible to expect that in the recession, as less-profitable firms go bankrupt and workers are layed off, private income as a whole will tend to decline. Assuming a lower limit, due to subsistence and habit-persistence reasons, to the decline in consumption, this would tend to result in an increasing share of consumption to private income, which would tend to again boost economic activity. A smaller number of firms, emerging from the crisis, would tend to pursue the process towards SOMP, leading eventually to a new global crisis, and so on. Given the giant firm's ability to respond to reductions in effective demand by restricting output, the effects of each crisis will tend to be borne by the vast majority of the people, rather than by transnational capital. In this sense, it would hardly be surprising if the political reaction to the increasing inequalities and waste of resources by transnational capitalism were to grow, leading eventually to its demise. The ability of capitalist states to constrain capital from its self-destructive policies by acting as a collective capitalist, might tend to become increasingly slimmer due to the TNCs' bargaining power. The economic role of the capitalist state might, as a result, tend to be limited to the provision of the appropriate conditions for investment in international capital, and also the military backing necessary for the protection of TNCs' interests from the actions of host-ile states, when required.[13] International co-operation may in the end be the only means of managing global economic crises and restraining transnational capital in its self-destructive tendencies. Similarly, working-class international co-operation appears to be the only means of protecting the interests of the working people from (the excesses of) transnational capitalism.

An empirical analysis of the US and UK experience

It has been suggested so far that the tendency towards SOMP will tend to increase the part of private disposable income retained within the corporate sector and that, given the assumption of imperfect substitutability between corporate retentions and personal saving, the end product will be a secular tendency for the consumption to private disposable income share to decline. More generally, the tendency towards SOMP should give rise to an increasing share of corporate income (profits) to private income, which *ceteris paribus* should result in a tendency for both the retentions and dividends shares to increase. If firms took positive action to increase or decrease the long-run pay-out ratio, an increasing share of profits might be associated with declining retentions or dividends. In the former case the tendency towards underconsumption would tend to be mitigated due to such firms' policies. In the latter it would tend to be exacerbated. Finally, even if the share of profits is declining, due, for example, to the effects of bankruptcies, etc., in the recession outweighing the effects of SOMP and/or due to the latter ceasing temporarily, an underconsumptionist tendency would still operate for as long as the rate of decline of retentions is smaller than the rate of decline of dividends, *ceteris paribus*.

In Table 1, we examine some historical statistics for the US, 1920–39 and 1945–84. Both the choice of starting and the ending periods were determined by the availability of data. Columns (1) and (2) in Table 1 summarize the shares of corporate retentions (CORE) and dividends (DIV) to private disposable income (PRI), and their rates of change (1a) and (2a) respectively.[14] The sum of columns (1) and (2) gives column (4) the share of profits, while column (3) has the share of consumers' expenditure to PRI.[15] As we are interested in secular trends, we make no conscious attempt to capture here the potentially important effects of cyclical changes and focus on five-year averages for the period under examination.

Table 1 broadly supports the following story. Before the big crash of 1929, the shares of both CORE and DIV were increasing, from 5.15% and 4.30% in 1920/24, to 6.99% and 5.72% respectively in 1925/29. Accordingly the share of profits increased from 4.45% to 12.71% of PRI.

The rate of increase of CORE was just higher than that of DIV. The consumers' expenditure share in PRI fell in this period from 88.41% to 86.00%. The above picture changed dramatically during the recession. The share of dividends fell slightly during 1930/34, while the share of retentions fell by more than fourfold. Accordingly the share of profits declined. The dramatic decline in the CORE/PRI ratio 'coincided' with a sharp increase in the share of consumer expenditure, from 86.00% to 96.24%.

In the period following the great recession, 1935/39, the CORE/PRI ratio increased while that of dividends fell. Retentions increased by more than the fall in dividends, leading to an increase in the profit share. The consumers' expenditure share fell dramatically in this period. This story

Table 1. *Gross after-tax Corporate Retained Earnings, Dividends, Consumers' Expenditure and Profit Shares to Gross Private Disposable Income (PRI), 1920–39 and 1945–84, US*

	Corporate Retained Earnings (CORE) (1)	Rate of change of CORE % (1a)	Dividends (DIV) (2)	Rate of change of DIV % (2a)	Consumers' Expenditure (C) (3)	Profits (Π) (4)=(1)+(2)
1920/24	5.15	—	4.30	—	88.41	9.45
1925/29	6.99	26.3	5.72	24.8	86.00	12.71
1930/34	1.63	−328.8	5.60	−2.1	96.24	7.23
1935/39	5.85	72.1	5.39	−3.9	90.01	11.24
1945/49	9.16	36.1	3.26	−65.3	82.64	12.42
1950/54	9.37	2.2	3.40	4.1	83.60	12.77
1955/59	10.31	9.1	3.32	−2.4	82.38	13.63
1960/64	10.42	1.0	3.39	2.1	82.85	13.81
1965/69	11.24	7.3	3.35	−1.2	80.83	14.59
1970/74	10.59	−6.1	2.82	−18.4	80.69	13.42
1975/79	11.96	11.5	2.68	−5.6	82.35	14.64
1980/84	12.13	1.4	2.66	0	81.39	14.79

Definitions and sources

CORE, DIV, Π Undistributed Income, Dividends and Gross Trading Profits after taxation of companies and financial institutions, gross of depreciation and stock appreciation. 1920–28 data obtained from Brittain (1966) and Lambrinides (1972). 1929–73 data obtained from the US National Income and Product Accounts (NIPA) Statistical Tables, 1929–74. 1974–84 data obtained from the US Survey of Current Business, Various Issues. Π includes rent and income from abroad but excludes profits due abroad.
C Total Consumers' Expenditure on durable and non-durable goods. Sources as above.
PRI Personal Sector Disposable Income (PSDI) plus CORE. Sources as above.

was repeated in 1945/49. In 1950/54 both the CORE and DIV shares increased, the latter by more. The profit share accordingly increased further; and so did the consumers' expenditure share. In 1955/59 an increase in the CORE/PRI ratio combined with a (smaller) decline in the DIV/PRI ratio resulted in an increase in the profit share and a decline in that of consumers' expenditure. In 1960/64 an increase in the CORE/PRI ratio, combined with a higher increase in the DIV/PRI ratio, gave rise to a further increase in the profit share and a small increase in the consumer expenditure share. In 1965/69 an increase in the CORE share combined with a smaller decline in the DIV share led to an increase in the profit share. It coincided with a decline in the consumer expenditure share.

There appears to be another small change in the picture in the recent recession. In 1970/74 the share of CORE fell by less than the share of DIV and this led to a decline in the profit share. The consumers' expenditure share also declined slightly in this period. In 1975/79 the CORE share increased while that of DIV declined. The rate of change of CORE was higher, leading to an increase in the profit share, but the consumption expenditure share also increased in this period. Finally, in 1980/84 an increase in the CORE share associated with a very small decline in the DIV share led to an increase in the profit share. The consumer expenditure share in this period declined.

It follows from the above that, with one notable exception, 1975/79, increases in the CORE/PRI ratio combined with a smaller increase or a decline in the DIV/PRI ratio led to a decline in the consumer expenditure ratio, while a higher increase/decline in the DIV/PRI share than that of the CORE/PRI share led to an increase/decline in the consumers' expenditure share. It follows that out of 11 cases, our scenario is supported in 10. Given the multiplicity of factors affecting consumption/saving, changes in which might have given rise to the 1975/79 'abnormality', it is fair, we think, to conclude on the basis of the above that the data lend some support to our propositions concerning movements in the CORE, DIV profit, and consumers' expenditure shares.

More interesting for the purposes of our theoretical propositions are the secular trends. Here again the latter appear to support our suggestions. In particular, the CORE/PRI share shows a remarkable tendency to increase over time, from 5.15% in 1920/24, to 12.13% in 1980/84. During the whole period it only declined twice over its previous period, in 1930/34 and 1975/79, both times of severe recession. The DIV/PRI ratio, on the other hand, was increasing up to the 1929 recession, and then started declining slowly but steadily from 5.72% in 1930/34 to just 2.66% in 1980/84. The profit share was increasing during the whole period, with only two exceptions again, 1930/34 and 1975/79. The overall increase was from

9.45% in 1920/24 to 14.75% in 1980/84. Finally, the consumers' expenditure share declined from 88.41% in 1920/24 to a 80.69% low in 1970/74. It fell by nearly 2.5 percentage points during the 1925/29 period before the big crash, increased dramatically during the recession and started declining again, only showing an upwards tendency in 1975/79.

To summarize the findings so far, the data in Table 1 appear to support the proposition that there is a secular tendency of the CORE/PRI ratio and the profit share to increase during the whole period under examination in the US. This was interrupted only in periods of severe recession, and started operating again immediately afterwards. A secular tendency appears to exist for the consumers' expenditure share to decrease, which is also reversed only during the crisis, and starts operating again soon after the recession. In this sense the secular trends observed in Table 1 appear to be in line with our suggestions.

In Table 2, the above exercise is repeated for the UK periods 1920–38 and 1946–84, for which reliable data was available. In brief, before the 1930s both the CORE/PRI and the DIV/PRI shares appear to be on the increase. In particular an increase in the share of CORE to PRI from 4.69% in 1920/24 to 5.05% in 1925/29, combined with a higher proportionate increase in the share of DIV, resulted in an overall increase in the share of profits. The share of consumers' expenditure declined. During the recession 1930/34 a decline in the CORE/PRI ratio, combined with a smaller decline in the DIV/PRI ratio, resulted in a lower profit share. The consumption share increased. Following that, in 1935/38 an increase in the CORE/PRI share combined with a smaller increase in the DIV/PRI share led to an increasing profit share; the consumption share fell.

Following the war years, in the 1946/50 period a dramatic increase (over 1935/38) in the CORE/PRI ratio, combined with an even higher decline in the DIV/PRI share, led to a small decline in the profit share; the consumption share also fell. In 1951/55 the CORE/PRI ratio increased and the DIV/PRI ratio fell by a lower rate than the increase in the CORE/PRI ratio. The profit share increased while the consumption share fell. In 1956/60, an increase in the CORE/PRI ratio alongside a higher decline in the DIV/PRI ratio resulted in a small decrease in the profit share. The consumption share fell further. In 1961/65 the CORE/PRI share fell slightly and the DIV/PRI share increased, leading to a further increase in the profit share. The consumption share, however, fell further. Following this, a small decline in the CORE/PRI ratio in 1966/70, combined with a higher increase in the DIV/PRI ratio, resulted in a small increase in the profit share; the consumption share also increased slightly. In 1976/80, an increase in the CORE/PRI ratio, combined with a smaller decline in the DIV/PRI ratio, resulted in a further increase in the profit share; the

Table 2. *After-tax Gross Corporate Retained Earnings, Dividends, Consumers' Expenditure and Profits Shares to Gross Private Disposable Income (PRI), 1920–38 and 1946–84, UK*

	Corporate Retained Earnings (CORE) (1)	Rate of change of CORE % (1a)	Dividends (DIV) (2)	Rate of change of DIV % (2a)	Consumer Expenditure (C) (3)	Profits (Π) (4)=(1)+(2)
1920/24	4.69	—	10.05	—	95.85	14.74
1925/29	5.05	7.1	11.22	10.4	91.86	16.27
1930/34	3.08	−64.0	10.75	−4.4	92.99	13.83
1935/38	5.56	44.6	12.29	12.5	89.24	17.85
1946/50	10.29	46.0	7.27	−69.0	88.23	17.56
1951/55	12.16	15.4	6.90	−5.4	85.28	19.06
1956/60	12.57	3.3	6.29	−9.7	82.90	18.86
1961/65	12.53	0	8.13	22.6	79.88	20.66
1966/70	11.93	−5.0	9.00	9.7	79.92	20.93
1971/75	14.90	12.9	7.92	−13.6	75.54	22.82
1976/80	16.61	10.3	7.38	−7.3	72.26	23.99
1981/84	14.80	−12.2	9.51	28.9	74.73	24.31

Definitions and sources

CORE, DIV, Π Undistributed Income Dividends and Gross Trading Profits after taxation of companies and financial institutions before providing for depreciation and stock appreciation. 1920–55 data obtained from Feinstein (1972). 1956–84 data obtained from National Income and Expenditure, Blue Book, Various Issues and Economic Trends Annual Supplement, ETAS, 1985. 1920–55 data also includes rent and income from abroad but excludes profits due abroad (net of UK tax) and taxes due abroad.

C Total Consumers' Expenditure on durable and non-durable goods.

PRI Personal Sector Disposable Income (PSDI) plus CORE. PSDI obtained from ETAS, 1985.

consumption share fell further. Finally, in 1981/84, a decline in the CORE/ PRI ratio, combined with a higher increase in the DIV/PRI ratio, led to a further increase in the profit share and an increase in the consumption share.

It can be seen from Table 2 that, in all cases examined, declines in the CORE/PRI ratio combined with an increase or smaller proportionate decline in the DIV/PRI ratio give rise to an increasing consumption share. Similarly, all increases in the CORE/PRI ratio, combined with a decline or smaller increase in the DIV/PRI ratio, give rise to a decline in the consumption share. Two 'abnormalities' appear to exist. In 1925/29 the DIV/PRI proportionate increase is higher than that of the CORE/PRI share and still the consumption share falls. More importantly, in 1961/65, the CORE/PRI ratio basically remains constant, while the DIV/PRI ratio increases. Still the consumption share falls further. Although, as already suggested, such 'abnormalities' are not very surprising in face of the complexity of the relationships involved, the 1925/29 'abnormality' appears to be easily explained. It seems plausible to suggest that, while an increase in CORE is not associated with a decline in personal saving, an increase in DIV may not result in an equivalent increase in consumption due to the fact that households save part of their disposable income either discretionally or more importantly compulsorily through their participation in pension funds. As already explained, a part of DIV never actually reaches workers' pockets but it is retained within the corporate sector in the form of the net inflow in LAPF. Thus an increase in CORE coupled with a higher increase in DIV may be consistent with a declining consumption share.

Focussing on secular trends, it can be seen from Table 1 that the CORE to PRI ratio increased dramatically in the period under examination, from 4.69% in the 1920/24 period, to a maximum of 16.61% in 1976/80. It was increasing in the period up to the 1929 recession, it declined during the recession and started rising again thereafter. It then declined slightly in the 1960s, rose again in the 1970s and finally started declining again in the early 1980s. The DIV/PRI share was also increasing up to the 1929 recession and fell slightly during the recession. It increased in the 1934/38 period but essentially stabilized after the war, ranging between 6.3% and 9.5% but with no discernible trend.

Accordingly, the profit share was increasing virtually non-stop during the whole period, with one major exception, the early 1930s' recession. It appeared to have reached a plateau in 1935/50 (although there is not sufficient information to suggest this conclusively), and another during the 1950s. The overall increase was a dramatic near-10% of PRI, from 14.74% in the 1920/24 period to 24.31% in 1981/84. The consumption share was declining during 1920/80, with the exception of the recession years 1930/34. It started rising again in the early 1980s. From its maximum of 95.85% in 1920/24, it dropped dramatically to 72.26% in 1976/80, an overall decline of 23.5% of PRI.

A quick comparison of Tables 1 and 2 suggests the following. First, in both the US and the UK the CORE, DIV and thus the profit shares are increasing up to the 1929 recession and drop during the recession years. The decline in CORE is far more pronounced than that of DIV, suggesting a tendency by firms to attempt to keep dividends constant in the short run perhaps to avoid a decline in share prices. During the same period the consumption share is falling in both countries and increases during the recession years. All changes are far more dramatic in the UK than in the US, particularly so the CORE, profits and consumers' expenditure shares.

After the 1929 recession the CORE and profits shares tend to increase in both countries, although the trend is far less discernible during the 1951–70 UK period and the 1955–74 US period. The DIV share shows no discernible trend in the UK, while it is steadily declining in the US. Dividends appear to play a far less important role (quantitatively) in the US than in the UK. There is also a higher share of profits in the latter, in the 1981/84 period a near quarter of PRI as opposed to just over one-seventh of PRI in the US. In both countries the tendency of the consumption share to fall manifests itself, but it is far more pronounced in the UK. In fact, the US share shows a remarkable stability over the 20-year period 1945–64 and appears to be moving back to its old level in recent years after a near 2 percentage points drop during the 1965–74 decade.

Still, it is clear from Table 1 that the 'remarkable stability' during the 1945–64 US period is against a background of a near-6% decline since 1920, and coincides with the relative stability of the CORE share during this period. This and the other reasons given so far would not lend any support to notions of 'ultrarationality'. In the UK the tendency of the trend to reverse manifested itself during the early 1980s.

We suggested in chapter 3 that perhaps the most important reason for the introduction and growth of occupational pension funds in the US and the UK was the capitalists' attempt to sustain and perhaps enhance the aggregate level of shareholding. Through their shareholding, pension funds own a sizeable proportion of all corporate profits (retentions and dividends). As such ownership is often not even known to pension funds' participants, pension funds make it highly unlikely that workers will react to changes in CORE by reducing their personal saving. More importantly, however, pension-fund shareholding implies that part of the dividends paid out by the industrial sector are not received by households but rather by financial institutions which in their turn retain part of them in the form of

Table 3. *After-tax Net Inflow in Life Assurance and Pension Funds, Contractual Saving and Net Personal Saving Shares to Gross Private Disposable Income, 1970–83, US*

	Net Inflow in Life Assurance and Pension Funds (NILP) (1)	Contractual Saving (COSA) (2)
1970/74	3.67	14.26
1975/79	4.91	16.87
1980/83	5.64	17.67

Definitions and sources
NILP Total contributions to Life Assurance and Pension Funds (LAPF) plus profit income earned by the funds minus benefits paid and administrative expenses. Source, Derek Blades, OECD Economic Accounts and Statistics Division.
COSA   CORE plus NILP. Source as for CORE and NILP.

the net inflow in LAPF. In this sense pension-funds shareholding introduces another form of corporate saving in the picture, thus another potential source of decreases in effective demand. Movements in the net inflow in LAPF (NILP) are therefore worth analysing both for their effects on the CORE and profits shares but also for their own potential effects on the consumption share.

The problem with analysing NILP is that of data availability. Both in the US and the UK these series have only recently begun being published in the official statistics, a factor which restricts the time-span of our analysis. In Table 3, column (1), we summarize the share of NILP to Private Income for the 1970–83 period in the US. In column (2) we give the share of Contractual Saving (COSA), defined as the sum of the shares of CORE and NILP. In our framework the tendency towards SOMP leads to an increasing share of CORE and NILP, thus COSA, and this leads to a decline in the consumption expenditure share. It can be seen from Table 3 that the NILP share was increasing in the period under examination, overall by nearly 2 percentage points from the 1970/74 period to the 1980/83 one. The overall COSA share as a result increased in this period by nearly 3.5 percentage points.

Table 4. *After-tax Net Inflow in Life Assurance and Pension Funds, Contractual Saving and Net Personal Saving Shares to Gross Private Disposable Income, 1951–84, UK*

	Net Inflow in Life Assurance and Pension Funds (*NILP*) (1)	Contractual Saving (*COSA*) (2)
1951/55	2.91	15.07
1956/60	3.52	16.09
1961/65	4.06	16.59
1966/70	4.07	16.00
1971/75	5.21	20.11
1976/80	6.01	22.67
1981/84	6.41	21.21

Definitions and sources
NILP Total contributions to LAPF plus profit income earned by LAPF minus benefits paid and administrative expenses. Source, Mike Sherring, UK Central Statistical Office.
COSA *CORE* plus *NILP*. Source as for *CORE* and *NILP*.

In Table 4 we repeat the previous exercise for the UK. In this case we obtained data on NILP since 1951, which allows a more detailed analysis. It can be seen from Table 4 that the NILP share was increasing virtually non-stop since 1951. Between 1951/55 and 1981/84 it more than doubled. Importantly it increased from the 1956/60 to the 1961/85 period, which provides a partial explanation for the decline in the consumption share during 1961/65. Overall, the contractual saving ratio increased from 15.07% in 1951/55 to 22.67% in 1976/80, although it was fairly stable during 1956/70. It started declining in 1981/84.

Tables 3 and 4 appear to confirm our suggestions of a tendency of the COSA share to increase secularly both in the US and the UK. More importantly they lend some support to our suggestions that the introduction and expansion of occupational pension funds schemes would facilitate the tendency of the CORE share to increase and that in doing so the share of NILP would tend to increase over time, leading to further declines in the share of consumers' expenditure. It is interesting that in both countries the tendency of the CORE share to increase in the 1970s and 1980s after a period of relative stability, coincided with the tendency of the NILP share to increase.

In the above scenario, the observed underconsumptionist tendency in the US and the UK was explained in terms of the impact of SOMP on the share of COSA in PRI, given less than perfect substitutability between COSA, on the one hand, and households' discretionary personal saving, on the other. An alternative scenario akin to the neoclassical theory would be that changes in factors affecting consumers' preferences tend to increase the share of discretionary saving to households' personal income and this tends to result in a decline in the consumption share. If this is true, an underconsumptionist tendency might be consistent with the neoclassical theory. Indeed, in recent years, there has been wide speculation and debate over the so-called 'paradox of saving', i.e. the tendency of the personal sector saving to the personal sector disposable income ratio to increase dramatically particularly in the early seventies in the US and up to 1980 in the UK. This tendency might appear to lend support to the neoclassical interpretation of events.

A number of hypotheses have been advanced to explain the above 'paradox of saving'. The idea that assumed prominence is that the high levels of inflation observed during the period of rising saving contributed to the increase in the personal saving ratio. Deaton (1977), for example, suggested that unanticipated inflation tends to lead to a mass illusion. Households tend to confuse relative price changes with absolute price changes, and adjust their consumption downwards, believing that only the prices of their planned purchases have increased. An alternative route through which inflation might affect saving is the suggestion that individuals holding money assets may realize that inflation tends to decrease the value of such assets. As a result, they may try to compensate for such losses by increasing their personal saving, see e.g. Townend (1976), Aaronovitch and Smith (1981). Deaton's evidence provided support to a positive impact of inflation on saving, as did a number of other studies, e.g. Townend (1976), Davidson et al. (1978), Hendry and von Ungern-Sternberg (1980).

In the US the personal saving ratio declined dramatically after 1975 while inflation was still increasing. This raised a question mark over the presumed effects of inflation on saving, see Peek (1983). More importantly it was soon observed that if inflation was affecting the behaviour of households, the appropriate saving variable to use was not that of personal sector saving, which Deaton and others used, but rather the discretionary saving of the households. Using such a measure, Cuthbertson (1983) identified a small positive impact of inflation on saving and concluded that previous studies exaggerated their case.

Other explanations of the 'saving paradox' include the role of capital gains, see Peek (1983), and the potential adverse effects of the uncertainty over future incomes due to the recession, on the purchase of durables, see Steindl (1982). One could also suggest that if inflation has an effect on saving, this may be through contributing to increasing the uncertainty over future incomes, as suggested by Steindl. Arguably, the most important product of the discussion on the 'paradox of saving', however, was an attempt to derive measures of households' truly discretionary income and saving. It is well known, for example, that the official definitions of personal sector saving include the income of unincorporated enterprises, as well as NILP and other contractual types of saving such as repayments of mortgages and other borrowing. Excluding such contractual types of saving from the definition of saving, Kennally (1985) found that in the UK the share of discretionary saving to personal sector disposable income was on average very close to zero and showed no discernible trend during the whole 1973–83 period. At its peak in 1980 it reached a maximum of 2.3 % of PSDI and then started declining, becoming negative in 1983. This dissaving was basically financed through increased borrowing on mortgages and consumer credit.[16]

Although we are not aware of a study of comparable detail to the above for the US, Blades (1983) provides a wealth of alternative measures of saving, which allow some interesting inferences. Excluding, for example, unincorporated enterprises from the definition of PSS and PSDI, Blades found that the adjusted ratio was only 61 % of the unadjusted for the period 1970–80, under the assumption of zero net saving (quasi-retentions) of the unincorporated sector. Adjusting PSS and PSDI for NILP, on the other hand, he found an adjusted ratio of 76 % of the unadjusted for the 1970–78 period. Blades' assumption of zero 'quasi-retentions' is, on his own admission, very conservative. One could assume that unincorporated business have a 'quasi-retention' ratio similar to that of the corporate sector, or even higher given that their problems in obtaining external finance are certain to be bigger than the corporate sector's. This would reduce further this adjusted household saving ratio. The latter would obviously be reduced further if other types of contractual saving were excluded from the definition of PSS.

The above lend some support to our earlier propositions that discretionary household saving may be little more than a transient phenomenon and in any case very close to zero. Changes in the discretionary saving to income ratio, mainly financed through borrowing, may in the short run tend to mitigate a tendency towards underconsumptionism, but in the longer run this is highly unlikely. Instead, changes in the importance of the unincorporated sector and 'quasi-retentions' may affect the underconsumptionist tendency, but the direction of this effect is not a priori obvious. It is possible, for example, that 'quasi-retentions' will increase following an increase in CORE and NILP, as small businesses try to compete by retaining more of their profits. In this case the underconsumptionist tendency would tend to be accentuated.

Although reliable data on 'quasi-retentions' is not available, there is some evidence that the trend in the importance of the unincorporated sector was different between the US and the UK. The proportion of self-employed persons to non-agricultural civilian employment in the former declined from 11% in 1960/64 to 7% in 1973–79. It rose again to 8% in 1980/82. In contrast, in the UK the respective ratios were 6%, 7% and 8%. This move towards self-employment in the UK might have resulted in a higher proportion of quasi-retentions, which might have accentuated the underconsumptionist crisis. At the same time in the US the trend was different, partly mitigating the crisis.

The conclusion to be drawn from the above discussion is that even from a purely quantitative point of view the observed underconsumptionist tendency in the US and the UK cannot be explained purely in terms of changes in factors affecting consumers' preferences. However important such factors may be, they only affect a small proportion of total private saving. Further, it is the exact multiplicity of such factors that makes any predictions on the discretionary saving to income ratio difficult. It is plausible that in some cases changes in the discretionary saving ratio will tend to mitigate an underconsumptionist tendency but in some others to accentuate it. It would appear more plausible to suggest that the SOMP induced underconsumptionist tendency was more severe in the UK, partly because of the impact of the increasing importance of the unincorporated sector in this country, relative to the US, and its effects on 'quasi-retentions', *ceteris paribus*.

It has been suggested that the underconsumptionist tendency would tend to increase excess capacity, which in its turn would put limits to potential increases on the profit rates due to the impact of SOMP on the profit share. Thus private investment would fail to fully compensate for decreases in the consumption share leading to a realization failure in the form of 'excess capacity' and 'excess saving'. *Ceteris paribus*, this would induce firms to undertake foreign operations which, depending on its degree and nature, might tend to offset or accentuate the crisis. The state might intervene but the potential impact of its alternative policies would not appear to offer an easy solution to the problem of realization failure, especially in a world characterized by a high level of internationalization of production and its associated importance of the transnational corporation.

In Table 5, we summarize some US data on 'excess capacity' in all manufacturing and the shares of gross private investment and 'excess saving' to PRI, for the 1960–74 period, during which the recent decline in

Table 5. *Gross Private Investment – 'Excess Saving' shares to Gross Private Disposable Income in constant 1972 US prices and Excess Capacity all Manufacturing, 1960–74*

	Gross Private Investment (GPI) (1)	'Excess Saving' (ES) (2)	'Excess Capacity' (EC) (3)
1960/64	15.25	1.90	16.40
1965/69	17.29	1.88	13.20
1970/74	15.45	3.86	22.20

Definitions and sources
GPI US Private Investment gross of Private Sector's Depreciation in constant 1972 US prices. Obtained from US NIPA, 1929–74, Statistical Tables.
ES One minus the sum of GPI and C. Sources as for GPI and C, in constant 1972 US prices.
EC The output/capacity ratio for all US Manufacturing. Obtained from the OECD Economic Outlook, various issues.

the consumption share was observed. It can be seen that 'excess capacity' declined between 1960/64 and 1965/69, but increased dramatically in the following period.[17] The share of private investment to PRI increased between 1960/64 and 1965/69 and declined afterwards. The share of 'excess saving' remained virtually stable between 1960/64 and 1965/69 but increased dramatically to 3.86% in the 1975/79 period.

Table 5 is in line with the existing evidence on the existence of a negative relationship between excess capacity and investment, see Cowling (1982) for a survey. In Table 5 decreases/increases in excess capacity are associated with increases/decreases in the share of private investment. It is also consistent with the idea that reductions in consumer expenditure would lead to increases in excess capacity for the 1965/69–1970/74 period, but not for the period 1960/64–1965/69. Still, the latter does not necessarily contradict our suggestions, given the potentially important effects on capacity utilization of the Vietnam War overheating during this period, 1966–68, see Bleaney (1985).

In Table 6, similar UK data is surveyed for the 1966–80 period, during which the last dramatic decline in the consumption share was observed. It can be seen that, unlike the US experience, in the UK excess capacity was increasing during the whole period under examination, from 5.52% in 1966/70 to 16.38% in 1976/80. The share of private investment was virtually stable during the whole period, thus failing to offset the decline in the consumption share. Accordingly, 'excess saving' increased dramatically

Table 6. *Gross Private Investment – 'Excess Saving' shares to Gross Private Disposable Income, in constant 1980 UK prices, and Excess Capacity all Manufacturing, 1966–80*

	Gross Private Investment (*GPI*) (1)	'Excess Saving' (*ES*) (2)	'Excess Capacity' (*EC*) (3)
1966/70	15.33	4.75	5.52
1971/75	15.16	9.30	12.60
1976/80	15.52	12.22	16.38

Definitions and sources
GPI   UK Private Investment gross of depreciation, in constant 1980 UK prices. Obtained from the UK National Income and Expenditure Blue Book, various issues.
ES   One minus the sum of *GPI* and *C*. Sources as for *GPI* and *C*, in constant 1980 UK prices.
EC   The output/capacity ratio for all UK Manufacturing. Obtained from Cowling (1982, 1985).

from 4.75% in 1966/70 to 12.22% in 1976/80. It follows that the UK experience is fully in line with our proposed suggestions.

Assuming that the capacity utilization of all manufacturing is not very different from that of the private sector as a whole, and multiplying the rate of capacity utilization by the share of profits, we can obtain the private disposable rate of profits, consistent with a constant organic composition of capital. The thus defined rate of profit in the period under examination in the US increased from 11.54% in 1960/64 to 12.64% in 1965/69 and fell to 10.49% in 1970/74. In the UK it remained virtually stable at around 20% during the whole period under examination. The above trends in the profit rate are broadly consistent with our suggestions that excess capacity increases will tend to offset the increases in the share of profits resulting from SOMP, thus putting pressures on profitability and investment.

More important is that the above broad constancy in the disposable rate of profit was obtained under the assumption of a constant organic composition of capital. It is often noted in the existing literature that the organic composition of capital did tend to increase during the post-war period, see e.g. Mandel (1975), Aaronovitch and Smith (1981), Bleaney (1985), although no conclusive data series appear to exist, principally due to the well-known problems associated with the measurement of capital stock. Supposing such an increasing tendency in the organic composition of capital did take place, our data would be consistent with a declining profit rate.

There is wide reference in the literature and evidence for a declining rate of profit in most capitalist countries in the post-war period, see e.g. Hill (1976) and Chan-Lee and Sutch (1985), which combined with our data might be taken to lend indirect support to the increasing organic composition of capital hypothesis, see, however, n. 8.[18] What is, we believe, of interest is the coincidence that the overall impact of the effects of SOMP on the profit share and excess capacity, and thus the profit rate, fails to show any discernible trends in both the US and the UK, leaving changes in the organic composition of capital as the crucial determinant of the rate of profit. In this sense the underconsumption/declining rate of profit aspects of Marxian crisis theory are neatly complementing each other in a common framework.

Also consistent with our proposed scenario is the widely accepted view of a dramatic increase in the operation of transnational corporations in the post-war period, see e.g. Stopford and Dunning (1983) for some measures of this phenomenon. It has also been reported that, unlike most other advanced capitalist countries, in the UK increases in overseas sales took place mostly through direct foreign production and less by way of exports. Between the 1957/65 period, for example, an increase of 32% in UK overseas sales was achieved by a 12% increase in exports and 20% in direct overseas production, see Stafford (1983). In more recent years UK FDI virtually doubled between the 1979–81 period, while portfolio investment increased from 1 billion in the 1978/79 period to 6.2 billion in 1982, see Hillard (1985).

Insufficient as they are, the above data have been used to justify the view of a 'relative decline' of the UK. To the extent that one can attach any reliability to them (which is not self-evident) they may be taken to be in line with our propositions that the effects of realization failures on 'excess capacity', excess saving and profit rates would be an increase in the degree of internationalization of production, and that countries with more 'cosmopolitan' capital, in this case the UK, may suffer more.

The choice of policy adopted by most capitalist states in the recent recession was that of deflation, see Bleaney (1985) for a detailed analysis, save perhaps for the US. The latter's discretionary fiscal policy during the 1965/69 period was expansionary, providing an explanation to the decline in excess capacity and the increase in the share of private investment in this period. With the exception of 1975 it became restrictive between 1970 and 1978 and started being expansionary again during the 1979–82 period. In the UK, on the other hand, discretionary fiscal policy was expansionary for a brief span of the early 1970s and became restrictive since then. As Price and Chouraqui (1983) observed, the Conservative government in this country failed to reduce substantially the budget deficit, despite its stated commitment to the contrary, due to the 'adverse' effects on expenditure of built-in stabilizers, such as unemployment benefits.[19] Still, the overall impact of the more restrictive fiscal policy in the UK relative to that of the US may be another explanatory factor of its 'relative decline'.[20]

To summarize, I suggested that the tendency towards SOMP will tend to introduce a tendency towards a realization crisis in advanced capitalist countries. This latter will tend to induce firms to undertake international operations, which in their turn may tend to globalize the tendency towards SOMP and prolong the realization crisis. This scenario is broadly in line with the existing evidence for the US and the UK. The problem appears to have been more severe in the UK. The degree and nature of the international activities of British-based capital, the policies of the state and a number of institutional factors, such as the role of the unincorporated sector, appear to offer a partial explanation for this relatively higher severity.

Notes

1. The socialization of corporate ownership

1 Throughout this monograph the terms 'Joint Stock Company', and the 'modern corporation' are used synonymously to describe firms owned by the public at large through shareholding.

2 It should be noted, however, that the ownership of share is not equivalent to the physical ownership of a firm's capital, characteristic of the pre-JSC firms. Instead, ownership of a share implies a legal entitlement on the part of those holding such shares to a part of any potential 'surplus' generated in the firm by putting its assets to work, see e.g. Thompson (1977), Scott (1985).

3 Throughout we use the terms SOCO and SOMP interchangeably to refer to a tendency towards an increasing participation of a country's people in the ownership of corporate shares, either voluntarily or compulsorily, e.g. through their participation in pension fund schemes. As will be detailed in the chapters that follow, the appearance and growth of the occupational pension fund schemes has resulted in a concentration of the control of corporate ownership in the hands of a few financial institutions and/or industrial firms, which control the pension funds. Still, by virtue of the fact that the ultimate beneficiaries of the pension fund are their participants, pension-fund shareholding represents an extension of the tendency towards SOMP to working people.

4 Throughout, we focus on what we consider to be the dominant view within a particular school of thought. Whenever more than one dominant view appear to exist, we attempt to account for them all.

5 According to Keynes' fundamental psychological law, for example, 'men are disposed ... to increase their consumption as their income increases, but not by as much as the increases of their income' (Keynes, 1973, p. 96).

2. Corporate control, corporate ownership

1 In this section we simply focus on what we view as the most interesting and/or significant contributions on the issue. More extensive discussions are in Nichols (1969) and Scott (1985).

2 Hilferding uses the term 'capitalists' here to encompass both controlling capitalists and small-level shareholders. It is in order to avoid such misleading usage that we suggested focussing on those with a controlling shareholding as the *differentia specifica* of the 'capitalist class'.

3 Marx suggested that capitalists may now be more risk prone, as they endanger only part of their own money. For Hilferding the interests of the non-controlling shareholders may act as a constraint on capitalists' greediness for profits.

4 For a detailed description of these and other theories of the firm, see Sawyer (1979).

5 Gordon suggested that emphasis on profit maximization may be less under managerial control rather than under owner control. For Berle and Means the controlling (managerial) group, even if they are owners themselves, can serve their pockets better by making profits at the expense of the company rather than for the company. This latter observation, of what Williamson (1964) called discretionary profits, is a very important aspect of the separation of (parts of) ownership from the 'unity' ownership and control in today's firms. Among others, it raises the important questions of the exact definition of profits, given that discretionary profits constitute unreported profits, and of the associated issue of the controlling group's consumption within the corporation rather than without it, see chapter 4. Our concern here, however, is not the undisputed existence of discretionary expenditures by the controllers of a firm, but rather the *assumption* that the latter are non-shareholder managers.

6 The very fact that the concentration of capital possessed by financial institutions is far higher than that possessed by the vast majority of households makes it distinctly possible that industrial capitalists may lose their control to financial capitalists, if they choose to borrow from the latter. In this sense the appearance of the joint stock company can be seen partly as the result of the difference in interests between industrial and financial capitalists.

7 Albeit it is often used as an argument for managerial control given that in a static *ex-post* sense managers are insiders!

8 Viz., Marx (1959) quoting Aristotle: 'Whenever the masters are not compelled to plague themselves with supervision, the managers assume *this honour*, while the masters attend to affairs of the state or study philosophy' (Vol. 3, p. 385, mockery in the original).

9 Such cases are widely reported in the existing literature, see e.g. Nyman and Silberston (1978), Herman (1979).

10 It is worth emphasizing that our point here is not that capitalists will always have full information, but simply that they will not be expected to act so irrationally as to not make sure that they have information enough to understand whether their decisions are being implemented or not, especially given that it is up to them to do so originally. Further, in the exceptional case where they do find themselves with insufficient information, one would expect them to try to acquire it, given that what is at stake is their control of the firms. In this sense managerial control may be an exceptional passing phenomenon, see also note 13 below.

11 Such pre-emptive behaviour is both theoretically plausible and well supported by the available evidence. Marglin (1982), for example, reports cases of capitalists ensuring the specialization on specific tasks not only of their workers but also of their managers, so that they retain for themselves the knowledge and functions of what they viewed as the most important aspects of the job.

12 The additional issue of death duties is raised in this case. Death duties may tend to break some estates (although the evidence for the UK does not appear to support such a scenario, see Hannah, 1976), and perhaps as a result lead to

liquidation of some firms. This will simply imply that control of the firms will be lost totally, which obviously is not to say that it will pass to managers.

13 It is in this sense as well that control by non-capitalist managers can only be – if anything – a passing phenomenon; since, if exceptional cases of such control ever appear, managers will try to make sure that their control is established by buying sufficient shares to warrant such control, i.e. by becoming capitalists.

14 The use by the controlling capitalists of methods such as voting and non-voting shares, preference shares and rights issues strengthens the above argument, see Aaronovitch (1961).

15 As already noted in Baran and Sweezy (1967), the power of small-level shareholders on the behaviour of the controlling shareholders should not be overlooked. However, restraining the behaviour of the controllers is a far cry from actually being in control, unless it can also be shown that such constraints are strong enough to ensure that, in the case of controlling and noncontrolling shareholders having conflicting interests, the controlling shareholders will always act to satisfy the non-controlling shareholders' interests and not their own, due to the latters' power.

16 Reference here is made to the labour theory of value and its associated idea that 'surplus value' is produced only by industrial companies while the existence of financial ones depends on them being able to share part of this 'surplus value'. See, however, Minns (1981) and our discussion in chapter 3.

17 By constraining management's discretion, in particular as regards profitability, the M-form may also result in increasing the management's 'control over the workforce'. Such 'control' may thus be seen *ex-ante* as an alternative explanation for the emergence of the M-form, see Marginson (1985).

3. Shareownership and 'social' choice

1 Our focus here is on what we consider as the dominant view of a broad school of thought. There is little doubt that both dissenting views within each school and some overlappings between the schools exist.

2 Incidentally, this 'simple' model introduced for the first time in the consumption function what was to become well known later, in the work of Davidson *et al.* (1978), as the 'error correction mechanism', see chapter 4.

3 An alternative interpretation of Marglin's views could be that 'capitalists' in his definition are simply the 'nominal owners of capital', e.g. small-level shareholders, in which case his 'management' may be taken to comprise large-scale shareholders and high-level managers, our view here. The above, however, is by no means obvious in Marglin's work. The adoption of a managerialist terminology, on the other hand, is in itself a reflection of the wide acclaim the managerialist position gained, even among Marxist writers; it resulted in the rather misleading (considering the differences) term 'Marxist-managerialists' as descriptive of the ideas advanced in particular by Baran and Sweezy, see e.g. Fitch (1972).

4 There is evidently a potential problem of aggregation in the above analysis. Some capitalists may not exhibit the same degree of preference for the retention ratio as others. In such cases, one should expect that capitalists who, for example, find the retention ratio 'excessive', would reduce their personal saving in order to reach their preferred consumption/saving to income ratio. Given their wealth, and (thus) access to borrowing, capitalists would be expected to

face few problems in doing so. The capitalist private saving to income ratio, that is, would express the desires of all capitalists, i.e. the result of a consensus outcome between capitalists. This is obviously the neoclassical position but applied only to the capitalists.

5 This is in line with the Marxist political analysis of capitalist societies, according to which such societies are real democracies for the ruling capitalists but essentially (concealed) dictatorships for the other societal classes, workers in particular.

6 In recent years the actual number of participants declined slightly, but the overall proportion increased due to increases in unemployment.

7 'Vesting' refers to the idea that a participating employee acquires a 'vested interest' in a pension only after a number of years at work. Before then, one cannot, for example, attempt to draw out the money, borrow against it, or assign one's interest. Full vesting exists only if an early leaver is fully entitled to preserve one's rights on change of employer.

8 The importance that industrial capitalists attribute to finance through retained earnings is highlighted in a statement by the chairperson of Unilevers, quoted in Aaronovitch (1961), according to which '... we think it most important to have large funds of our own, because we cannot always be certain of being able to raise money on the market when opportunities present themselves' (p. 159).

9 For the pure version of the substitution hypothesis to be true, Feldstein (1978) suggests, one should assume *inter alia* correct employee perception, constant employee total asset accumulation and full funding.

10 Discretionary saving in Kennally's definition excludes from personal sector saving not only committed saving in LAPF, but all other committed saving as well, see chapter 5.

11 Most of the evidence along these lines has been obtained within the framework of the Life Cycle Hypothesis, see chapter 4, appropriately extended to include a corporate retentions and/or a pension funds variable so as to test the effects of the latter on personal saving/consumption. Such extensions have been named by Feldstein (1973, 1978) the extended Life Cycle Hypothesis. We examine the evidence here by assuming that the results of all surveyed studies are reliable. This need not always be the case but a detailed critique of each particular study is well beyond the scope of this monograph.

4. The saving function

1 See Kalecki (1971) and Rowthorn (1981). Note, however, that some post-Kaleckians, e.g. Sawyer (1982), adhere to versions of the neo-Keynesian Saving Function, see below.

2 It has been suggested that the riskier character of profits idea overlooks the uneasy coexistence of relatively safer types of profit income, e.g. rent and interest, with the 'riskier' dividends and profits from self-employment, Hacche (1979).

3 The importance of this 'shift' in emphasis by Kaldor was also acknowledged by Pasinetti (1983), who originally (Pasinetti, 1962) proposed a correction of equation (1) to account for profits accruing to workers.

4 The convergence in the form of the MSF should thus not mask the often important differences in the perspective of its various proponents. For example, what for Kregel is a mythical property-owning democracy, for Galbraith and Marglin appears to describe accurately our real world.

5 The studies summarized above may differ in many respects, one being their definition of 'transfers' as wage income or their identification as a separate income category. A more detailed discussion on this issue is in Pitelis (1984). Suffice it to note here that this discussion does not change the qualitative nature of our conclusion.

6 This model expresses the change in consumption as a function of the change in disposable income and a one-period lagged saving variable, see Appendix. The aim of the latter in Davidson *et al.* (1978) is to ensure consistency with the theoretical proposition that in the 'long run' the propensity to consume is equal to one, thus the term 'error correction'. For Marglin (1975) the lagged saving variable attempts to capture households' process of learning to adjust their consumption to their disposable income, in the short run.

7 Ideally this would require the estimation of two saving functions; one for capitalists and one for the non-controlling sectors of the population.

8 Following standard official statistics conventions, NPS thus defined includes the saving of unincorporated businesses, 'quasi-retentions', as well as expenditure on housing. It excludes durable goods which are considered to be consumption. For a measure of truly discretionary NPS one should exclude 'quasi-retentions' from it, and similarly adjustments should be made to account for repayment of mortgages. Although attempts have been made in recent years to devise such measures of NPS, see Cuthbertson (1983), Kennally (1985), they only cover a relatively short period of time. In this sense our use of NPS measures not only how households react to changes in CORE and/or NILP but also whether 'quasi-retentions' and contractual repayments of mortgages react to such changes.

9 Alternatively (A) implies that, with constant real NPDI, no household saving would exist, see the Appendix, pp. 75–76.

10 Whenever testable differences in the parameter values are implied by the mathematical form of the various models giving rise to (A), these can also be tested so as to derive the theory best supported by the data. This is not our aim here.

11 The treatment of 'transfers' as 'social wage' also fails to account for wider issues such as the argument that transfers can be viewed as a subsidy to capital. By being financed by taxes on the whole population, transfers socialize the cost of labour, which in their absence would be borne by the capitalists.

12 Some of the hypotheses consistent with (A) give rise to a one-period Moving Average (MA1) error term, and such tests could also be undertaken. Still, our assumption of AR1 here may be viewed as an approximation to MA1, see e.g. Townend (1977).

13 Note, however, that the inclusion of CORE and NILP in the dependent variable leads to a spurious increase in the explanatory power of the regressions.

14 It also partly accounts for a criticism by Feldstein (1978a) of Howrey and Hymans (1978) according to which the use of private Y and S is somehow better than that of net Y and S. In our equations 1.5 and 1.6 the assumption that CORE and NILP are exogenous to the households leads to PRSA becoming the dependent variable but lagged NPS being left in the right-hand side of the equations. This marries the use of private and net personal sector data. It also emphasizes the important point that our tests here assume that CORE and NILP are exogenous to the household sector and that separate models should be developed to examine how they are determined, see e.g. Hart (1968) and Furstenberg (1981) for the case of CORE. If this is done then a private saving

function can be estimated including the determinants of all NPS, CORE and NILP. To use PRSA and PRI as in the LCH, without first having accounted for the determinants of CORE and NILP, is equivalent to assuming that NPS, CORE and NILP are all determined by the same factors; a hypothesis that needs to be tested rather than assumed.

15 The problem with this treatment is that WI includes the profit income of the LAPF, which clouds the correspondence between type of income and income receiver. It is worth noting that workers' profits through pension funds provide a justification to Pasinetti's (1962) interest in profit income earned by workers. Our results here as a result test an amalgam of the 'Kaldorian' hypothesis (1) and its Pasinettian (1962) version which accounts for workers' profits.

16 Other factors usually thought to affect consumption/saving include the rates of interest, inflation and unemployment, as well as capital gains and saving from social security schemes. The impact of the interest rate on consumption/saving is controversial both in theory, see e.g. Fisher (1965) and Marglin (1985), and in the existing evidence, see chapter 5.

   Similar is the case of the inflation rate, see Branson and Klevorick (1969), Deaton (1977) and our discussion in the next chapter. Unemployment may have a positive effect on saving. For example, by increasing uncertainty over future income, an increasing unemployment rate may induce some people to save more while still at work. The potential effects on capital gains on consumption/ saving have been examined in Arena (1964), Bhatia (1972) and Peek (1985). The results appear to be conflicting. Feldstein (1974) has suggested that the introduction of social security schemes in advanced capitalist countries might result in a decline in the total (national) saving in these countries. This position assumes perfect substitutability between personal saving and social security saving. It has been criticized, e.g. by Tobin (1980) for overlooking, *inter alia*, the possibility of liquidity constrained households. From a different point of view, Feldstein's position was also attacked by the proponents of the 'Rational Expectations Revolution', see e.g. Barro (1974), and the critique of this thesis by Tobin (1980). The extensive evidence on the 'Feldstein hypothesis' is inconclusive, see Kessler *et al.* (1981) for a survey. It was beyond our purposes in this chapter to account for all the above factors. Such an attempt in fact might have harmful rather than beneficial effects on our estimates; as it would reduce our degrees of freedom and thus impair the reliability of our results. Still, the fact that so many potential explanatory variables were not included in our regressions reinforces the suggestion that our results are more indicative rather than conclusive.

5. Capital accumulation and the realization of profits

1 As already pointed out, this change in the functional distribution of income need not necessarily result in a corresponding change in the size distribution of income, as it is possible that workers too buy shares, in particular via their participation in pension fund schemes.

2 In doing so, established firms may also raise barriers to potential entrants, thus restricting entry and reducing potential output, *ceteris paribus*.

3 An alternative scenario, more akin to neoclassical theorizing, would be to suggest that decreases in consumption (increases in saving) might tend to reduce interest rates and thus increase investment. The existing empirical literature

would not appear to lend support to this view. The relationship between saving and the interest rate is highly inconclusive, see e.g. Howrey and Hymans (1978) and Arestis and Driver (1980) for surveys of the US and UK evidence respectively. The presumed relation between the interest rate and investment, on the other hand, also appears to be tenuous. Two surveys of the existing evidence on the determinants of investment, Sawyer (1982) and Stafford (1983), suggest that capacity utilization and output are far more important determinants of investment than financial factors, e.g. interest rates.

4 In the 'reappraisal' model of Keynesian economics, see e.g. Muellbauer and Portes (1978), underconsumption is defined as a (static equilibrium) situation where overproduction coexists with excess demand for labour due to a very low wage rate. On the other hand, the coexistence of overproduction and unemployment due to excess supply in both the labour market and the goods market is characterized as 'Keynesian unemployment'. In the above classifications 'underconsumption' excludes the possibility of involuntary unemployment. In our framework, Keynesian underconsumption is a situation where changes in income distribution along with differential saving propensities result in lower consumption, investment and output, thus involuntary unempolyment. In this sense our definition of Keynesian underconsumption is closer to the definition of 'Keynesian unemployment' in the 'reappraisal' model.

5 This is in contrast to the limit-pricing model, see e.g. Modigliani (1958) in which the price-output decisions of the firms are 'constrained', in that they are taken with an eye to keeping potential entrants out of the industry.

6 For other criticisms of the Baran and Sweezy (1967) model, regarding both their views and data on the generation and absorption of the surplus, see Mandel (1967) and Bleaney (1976).

7 Theorists in the 'Monopoly Capital' tradition have been widely criticized for this 'individualistic' approach, reminiscent of the neoclassical methodology, and their apparent focus on the generation of profits in the process of exchange rather than in production, see Fine and Murfin (1984). It would appear to us, however, that critics have tended to overstate their case. The Baran and Sweezy–Cowling model can be freed from its 'individualism' as soon as it is accepted that the underlying reason for firms' behaviour is competition for the generation and appropriation of 'surplus value'. The focus on exploitation in the process of exchange, on the other hand, is not incompatible with exploitation in production. In fact the two, as Marx (1939) suggests, are inseparable. Surplus value is produced at the production level, but realized at the level of exchange. Higher prices as a result, due to monopolization of markets, increase the overall level of labour exploitation. There is nothing here to suggest that the latter does not take place in production.

8 The question as to whether Marx was an 'underconsumptionist' or not has become the subject of debate between authors mainly in the Marxist tradition. Sweezy (1942) and Steindl (1952) in particular regarded Marx as an 'underconsumptionist', while others, e.g. Glyn and Sutcliffe (1972), Bleaney (1976), reject this idea. Both sides are able to produce passages from Marx's writings which support their own case. For our purposes here the answer to the above question is of no importance. What is important, we think, is that in our framework underconsumption and rising organic composition of capital leading to declining profit rates can coexist. Note also that Marx's view that labour-saving technological progress leads to declining profit rates is not

universally accepted even among Marxist economists. This issue, however, is beyond the scope of this book.

9 It is possible to suggest that in the recession the rate of decline of actual profits due, for example, to bankruptcies will be higher than that of consumption, due to 'subsistence' and 'habit persistence' considerations. In this case the consumption share will tend to increase in the trough of the cycle, initiating a process of expansion. This would once more set in operation the tendency towards SOMP.

10 Excess capacity in saving is one of the reasons for FDI suggested by the 'specific advantage' hypothesis, see Koutsoyiannis (1982) for a survey of this and other theories of FDI. The role of underconsumption in 'imperialism' goes back to Luxemburg (1951); see also Baran and Sweezy (1967). Our intention here is not to deny the potentially many and complex factors entering a firm's decision to go abroad. Rather it is to emphasize that underconsumptionist tendencies and more generally macroconsiderations may well be of importance in taking this decision.

11 Note that the latter may be the very result of the operations of TNCs, given the latter's ability to separate workers into country-specific groups and thus increase their bargaining power relative to labour, see Sugden (1985).

12 For a detailed discussion of the political-economic problems of inflation, see Rowthorn (1977).

13 The ideologico-political functions of the state may also tend to increase, so as to legitimize the process of deflation.

14 We define corporate retentions gross of depreciation. Obviously some measure of wearing and obsolescence of a firm's fixed assets needs to be subtracted from the gross measure in order to reach a measure of net corporate retentions. There are, however, various problems in doing so. First, as already observed, depreciation allowances do not represent current outlays and, to the extent a firm's profits suffice to cover these provisions, they are used in order to finance investment. These need not necessarily involve projects for the replacement of fixed assets, see Wood (1975). Second, depreciation allowances may be higher than what is actually required for the replacement of fixed assets, e.g. for taxation purposes, see Lambrinides (1972). Third, measures of depreciation may differ from firm to firm in line with the depreciation rules applied by the firm's accountants. Thus a measure of net retained earnings may be less reliable than a measure of gross retained earnings, especially if one is interested in secular trends. Partly because of the above reasons the use of gross measure of CORE is the norm in Kalecki (1971) and others in this tradition, e.g. Wood (1975). Much of the above theorizing, however, is also accepted by some neoclassicals, e.g. Feldstein (1973).

15 The focus on after-tax CORE, 'profits' and PRI is motivated by the fact that, in buying corporate shares, individuals make use of their after-tax disposable income. Similarly, pension contributions are paid by workers simultaneously with their taxes' payment, representing a reduction in their after-tax income. For all those reasons our propositions are formulated in terms of secular trends of after-tax NILP and CORE on after-tax PRI. It should be obvious that in doing so the state is entering the picture indirectly, and in this sense our data also reflect partly the state's policies in, for example, relieving capitalists' pressures on profitability. It is indeed the case, for example, that in the recent recession profit taxes have declined steadily in most capitalist countries, see e.g.

Chan-Lee and Sutch (1985). It should also be noted that our measure of 'profits' here differs from our measure of 'property' income used in the previous chapter in that it does not include income from self-employment.

16 As noted, the very prospect of debts repayment as well as problems associated with borrowing make it unlikely that the latter will suffice to fully offset changes in CORE and NILP, even if it is assumed that households are fully aware of their ownership claims on the latter.

17 In particular, capacity utilization peaked in 1966 and started declining afterwards. The exact figures used here should be taken with a pinch of salt as they are taken from the OECD Economic Outlook *graphs* of capacity utilization.

18 Our data are not strictly comparable with the data provided in these sources for various reasons. More important is our focus on the private sector as a whole, our use of after-tax profit shares-rates and the fact that we include depreciation allowances in our definitions. Focussing on before-tax, gross of depreciation, profits of the total business sector as a ratio of the gross value added of this sector, Chan-Lee and Sutch (1985) obtained a positive but insignificantly different from zero trend for the 1960–82 period for the UK, and a small negative but significantly different from zero negative trend for the US. Profit rates trends, on the other hand, were found to be negative and significantly different from zero in both countries.

19 Another reason is the 'defence' expenditures. In the UK the proportion of such expenditure to GDP increased moderately in the 1973–83 period.

20 A number of other factors have been suggested to explain the recent crisis, e.g. the oil-price shocks in the 1970s. Although it is not to be denied here that such factors did have an impact on the (differential) performance of advanced capitalist countries it would appear to us naive to consider them as the source of the crisis, see Bleaney (1985) for a detailed discussion on this issue. It is obvious, e.g. from our data, that the underlying tendency towards crisis was present both in the US and the UK well before the appearance of such external shocks, which therefore should best be seen in our framework only as factors contributing to the crisis. It also seems worth emphasizing that our evidence in this chapter is not intended to be conclusive. First, due to the well-known problems regarding the general reliability of any data used, and the availability of data compatible with one's theoretical propositions. Second, an additional problem in our framework arises from the fact that, while our theoretical propositions are built in a stepwise fashion, i.e. from the private sector to the overseas sector and the state sector, in real life observed *ex-post* data have been subject to the influence of the behaviour of all sectors simultaneously.

References

Aaronovitch, S. (1961), *The Ruling Class*, Greenwood Press Publishers, Connecticut.

Aaronovitch, S. and Sawyer, M. (1975), *Big Business: Theoretical and Empirical Aspects of Concentration and Mergers in the U.K.*, London, Macmillan.

Aaronovitch, S. and Smith, R. (with Gardiner, I. and Moore, R.) (1981), *The Political Economy of British Capitalism: A Marxist Analysis*, McGraw-Hill Ltd., London.

Ando, A. and Modigliani, F. (1963), 'The Life Cycle Hypothesis of Savings: Aggregate Implications and Tests', *American Economic Review*, 53.

Arena, J. J. (1964), 'Capital Gains and the "Life Cycle" Hypothesis of Saving', *American Economic Review*, 54, 107–11.

Arestis, P. and Driver, C. (1980), 'Consumption out of Different Types of Income in the U.K.', *Bulletin of Economic Research*, Vol. 32.

Baran, P. A. (1962), *The Political Economy of Growth*, Monthly Review Press, New York.

Baran, P. and Sweezy, P. (1967), *Monopoly Capital*, Penguin Books.

Barro, R. J. (1974), 'Are Government Bonds Net Wealth?', *Journal of Political Economy*, Vol. 82, No. 6.

Baumol, W. J. (1959), *Business Behaviour, Value and Growth*, Macmillan.

Berle, A. J. and Means, C. G. (1967), *The Modern Corporation and Private Property*, Harcourt Brace and World, New York.

Bhatia, K. B. (1972), 'Capital Gains and the Aggregate Consumption Function', *American Economic Review*, 62, 866–79.

Bhatia, K. B. (1979), 'Corporate Taxation, Retained Earnings and Capital Formation', *Journal of Public Economics*, 11.

Blades, D. (1983), 'Alternative Measures of Saving', *OECD Economic Outlook, Occasional Studies*, June.

Bleaney, M. (1976), *Underconsumption Theories: A History and Critical Analysis*, Lawrence and Wishart, London.

Bleaney, M. (1985), *The Rise and Fall of Keynesian Economics*, Macmillan, London.

Blinder, A. J. (1975), 'Distribution Effects and the Aggregate Consumption Function', *Journal of Political Economy*, Vol. 83, No. 3.

Bliss, C. (1976), *Capital Theory and the Distribution of Income*, North Holland Publishing Company.

References

Botty, R. and Crotty, J. (1975), 'Class Conflict and Macro Policy', *Review of Radical Political Economics*, Spring.

Branson, W. H. and Klevorick, A. K. (1969), 'Money Illusion and the Aggregate Consumption Function', *American Economic Review*, 59, 832–49.

Brewer, A. (1980), *Marxist Theories of Imperialism*, Routledge and Kegan Paul.

Brittain, J. (1966), *Corporate Dividend Policy*, Brookings Institution.

Brown, T. F. (1952), 'Habit Persistence, and Lags in Consumer Behaviour', *Econometrica*, July.

Browning, J. M. (1982), 'Savings and Pensions: Some U.K. Evidence', *The Economic Journal*, December, 954–63.

Burmeister, E. and Taubman, P. (1969), 'Labour and Non-Labour Income Saving Propensities', *The Canadian Journal of Economics*, February, 79–89.

Burnham, J. (1962), *The Managerial Revolution*, Penguin Books.

Cagan, P. (1965), *The Effects of Pension Plans on Aggregate Saving: Evidence from a Sample Survey*, National Bureau of Economic Research, Occasional Paper 95.

Chan-Lee, J. H. and Sutch, H. (1985), 'Profits and Rates of Return', OECD Economic Outlook, December.

Coackley, J. and Harris, L. (1982), 'Evaluating the Role of the Financial System', *Socialist Economic Review*.

Cowling, K. (1982), *Monopoly Capitalism*, Macmillan.

Cowling, K. (1983), 'Excess Capacity and the Degree of Collusion: Oligopoly Behaviour in the Slump', *The Manchester School*, December.

Cowling, K. (1985), 'The Internationalization of Production and Deindustrialization', Warwick Economic Research Papers, 256.

Cubbin, J. and Leech, D. (1983), 'The Effect of Shareholding Dispersion on the Degree of Control in British Companies: Theory and Measurement', *Economic Journal*, June.

Cuthbertson, K. (1983), 'The Measurement and Behaviour of the U.K. Saving Ratio in the 1970's, *National Institute Economic Review*, February.

David, P. A. and Scadding, J. L. (1974), 'Private Savings: Ultrarationality, Aggregation and Denison's Law', *Journal of Political Economy*, Vol. 82, 225–49.

Davidson, J., Hendry, D., Srba, F. and Yeo, S. (1978), 'Econometric Modelling of the Aggregate Time-Series Relationship Between Consumers' Expenditure and Income in the United Kingdom', *The Economic Journal*, December, 661–92.

Davis, E. P. (1984), 'The Consumption Function in Macroeconomic Models: A Comparative Study', *Applied Economics*, December.

Deaton, A. (1977), 'Involuntary Savings Through Unanticipated Inflation', *American Economic Review*, December.

Denison, E. F. (1958), 'A Note on Private Saving', *The Review of Economics and Statistics*, Vol. XL, August, 261–7.

De Vroey, M. (1974), 'The Separation of Ownership and Control in Large Corporations', *Review of Radical Political Economics*, Vol II, No. 2.

Dicks-Mireaux, L. and King, M. (1983), 'Pension Wealth and Household Savings: Tests of Robustness', SSRC Programme in Taxation, Incentives and the Distribution of Income, No. 41, forthcoming *Journal of Public Economics*.

Dixit, A. (1976), *The Theory of Equilibrium Growth*, Oxford University Press.

Dobb, M. (1958), *Capitalism Yesterday and Today*, Lawrence and Wishart, London.

Drucker, F. P. (1976), *The Unseen Revolution: How Pension Fund Socialism Came to America*, Harper and Row, New York.

Duesenberry, J. S. (1967), *Income, Saving and the Theory of Consumer Behaviour*, New York, Oxford University Press.

Feinstein, C. H. (1972), *Statistical Tables of National Income, Expenditure and Output of the UK, 1855–1965*, Cambridge University Press.

Feldstein, M. (1973), 'Tax Incentives, Corporate Saving, and Capital Accumulation in the United States', *Journal of Public Economics*, 2, 159–71.

Feldstein, M. (1974), 'Social Security, Induced Retirement and Aggregate Capital Accumulation', *Journal of Political Economy*, 82.

Feldstein, M. (1978), 'Do Private Pensions Increase National Savings?', *Journal of Public Economics*, 10.

Feldstein, M. (1978a), 'Comments and Discussion' to the Howrey, E. P. and Hymans, S. H. paper, *Brookings Papers on Economic Activity*, 3, 686–90.

Feldstein, M. and Fane, G. (1973), 'Taxes, Corporate Dividend Policy and Personal Savings. The British Postwar Experience', *Review of Economics and Statistics*, Vol. LV.

Ferber, R. (1973), 'Consumer Economics: A Survey', *Journal of Economic Literature*, December.

Fine, B. and Murfin, A. (1984), *Macroeconomics and Monopoly Capitalism*, Wheatsheaf Books Ltd.

Fisher, I. (1965), *The Theory of Interest*, Augustus, M. Kelley, Bookseller, New York.

Fitch, R. (1972), 'Reply to James O'Connor', *Socialist Revolution*, 7.

Francis, A. (1980), 'Families, Firms and Finance Capital: the Development of the U.K. Industrial Firms with Particular Reference to their Ownership and Control', *Sociology*, Vol. 14.

Francis, A. (1980a), 'Company Objectives, Managerial Motivations and the Behaviour of Large Firms: an Empirical Test of the Theory of "Managerial" Capitalism', *Cambridge Journal of Economics*, 4.

Friedman, M. (1957), *A Theory of the Consumption Function*, Princeton, N.J., Princeton University Press.

Furstenberg, G. M. von (1981), 'Saving', in Aaron, H. J. and Pechman, J. A., eds., *How Taxes Affect Economic Behaviour*, The Brookings Institution.

Galbraith, J. K. (1967), *The New Industrial State*, Penguin Books.

Garvy, G. (1950), 'The Effect of Private Pension Plans on Personal Savings', *The Review of Economics and Statistics*, August, 223–6.

Gerth, H. H. and Mills, C. W. (1952), 'A Marx for the Managers', in Merton, R. K. et al. eds., *Reader in Bureaucracy*, The Free Press, New York.

Glyn, A. and Sutcliffe, B. (1972), *British Capitalism, Workers and the Profits Squeeze*, Harmondsworth, Penguin Books.

Gordon, A. P. (1952), 'The Executive and the Owner-Entrepreneur', in Merton, R. K. et al. eds., *Reader in Bureaucracy*, The Free Press, New York.

Green, F. (1981), 'The Effect of Occupational Pension Schemes on Saving in the United Kingdom: A Test of the Life Cycle Hypothesis', *Economic Journal*, March, 136–44.

Green, F. (1982), 'Occupational Pension Schemes and British Capitalism', *Cambridge Journal of Economics*, 6, 267–83.

Green, H. A. J. (1971), *Consumer Theory*, Penguin Books.

Hacche, G. (1979), *The Theory of Economic Growth. An Introduction*, St Martin's Press Inc.

Hannah, L. (1976), *The Rise of the Corporate Economy*, Methuen, London.

Harrod, R. (1948), *Towards a Dynamic Economics*, Macmillan.

Hart, P. E. (1968), *Studies in Profit, Business, Saving and Investment in the United Kingdom, 1920–1962*, Vol. 2, George Allen and Unwin Ltd, London.

Harvey, A. C. (1981), *The Econometric Analysis of Time-Series*, Philip Allan Publishers Ltd.

Hay, D. A. and Morris, D. J. (1979), *Industrial Economics: Theory and Evidence*, Oxford University Press.

Hemming, R. and Harvey, R. (1983), 'Occupational Pension Scheme Membership and Retirement Saving', *Economic Journal*, March, 128–44.

Hendry, D. F. (1983), 'Econometric Modelling: The "Consumption Function" in Retrospect', *Scottish Journal of Political Economy*, June.

Hendry, D. and Ungern Sternberg, T. von (1980), 'Liquidity and Inflation Effects on Consumers' Expenditure', in Deaton, A. S., *Essays in the Theory and Measurement of Consumer Behaviour*, Cambridge University Press.

Herman, E. S. (1979), *Corporate Control, Corporate Power*, Cambridge University Press.

Hilferding, R. (1981), *Finance Capital*, Routledge and Kegan, London.

Hill, T. P. (1979), *Profits and Rates of Return*, OECD.

Hillard, J. (1985), 'Thatcherism and Decline', in Coates, D. and Hillard, J., eds., *The Economic Decline of Modern Britain*, Wheatsheaf Books Ltd.

Hobsbawm, E. J. (1969), *Industry and Empire*, Pelican.

Holbrook, R. and Stafford, F. (1971), 'The Propensity to Consume Separate Types of Income: A Generalized Permanent Income Hypothesis', *Econometrica*, January.

Houthakker, H. S. and Taylor, L. D. (1970), *Consumer Demand in the United States 1919–1970: Analyses and Projections*, Harvard University Press.

Howrey, E. P. and Hymans, S. H. (1978), 'The Measurement and Determination of Loanable-Funds Saving', *Brookings Papers on Economic Activity*, 3, 655–85.

Jessop, B. (1977), 'Recent Theories of the Capitalist State', *Cambridge Journal of Economics*, 1.

Kaldor, N. (1960), *Essays on Value and Distribution*, Duckworth Ltd.

Kaldor, N. (1966), 'Marginal Productivity and Macro-Economic Theories of Distribution', *Review of Economic Studies*, Vol. 33.

Kalecki, M. (1971), *Dynamics of the Capitalist Economy*, Cambridge University Press.

Katona, G. (1965), *Private Pensions and Individual Saving*, Monograph No. 40, Survey Research Center, University of Michigan.

Kennally, G. (1985), 'Committed and Discretionary Saving of Households', *National Institute Economic Review*, May.

Kessler, D., Masson, A. and Strauss-Kahn, D. (1981), 'Social Security and Saving: A Tentative Survey', *The Geneva Papers on Risk and Insurance*, 18, January.

Keynes, J. M. (1936), *The General Theory of Employment, Interest and Money*, Macmillan, London.

Kilpatrick, A. and Lawson, T. (1980), 'On the Nature of Industrial Decline in the UK', *Cambridge Journal of Economics*, March.

Klein, L. R. (1950), *Economic Fluctuations in the United States, 1921–1941*, John Wiley and Sons, New York.

Klein, L. R., Ball, R. J., Hazlewood, A. and Vandome, P. (1961), *An Econometric Model of the U.K.*, Oxford, Blackwell.

Klein, L. R. and Goldberger, A. (1955), *An Econometric Model of the U.S.*, North Holland Publishing Company.

Koutsoyiannis, A. (1982), *Non Price Decisions*, Macmillan, London.

Kregel, J. A. (1971), *Rate of Profit, Distribution and Growth: Two Views*, Macmillan.

Lambrinides, M. (1972), 'Saving, Distribution and Social Choice: A Study of the Relationship Between Personal and Organisational Saving', Unpublished Ph.D. Thesis, Harvard University.

Leech, D. (1984), 'The Separation of Corporate Ownership and Control: A Reinterpretation of the Evidence by Berle and Means', Warwick Economic Research Papers, No. 247.

Luxemburg, R. (1951), *The Accumulation of Capital*, Routledge and Kegan Paul Ltd, London.

Mandel, E. (1967), 'The Labour Theory of Value and "Monopoly Capitalism"', *International Socialist Review*, July–August.

Mandel, E. (1967a), 'Surplus Capital and the Realization of Surplus Value', *International Socialist Review*, July–August.

Mandel, E. (1975), *Late Capitalism*, Verso Edition, London.

Marginson, P. (1985), 'The Multidivisional Firm and Control Over the Work Process', *International Journal of Industrial Organization*, 3.

Marglin, S. (1975), 'What Do Bosses Do? The Origins and Functions of Hierarchy in Capitalist Production', Part II, *Review of Radical Political Economics*, Winter.

Marglin, S. (1975a), 'What Do Bosses Do? Postscript', Harvard Institute of Economic Research, Discussion Paper No. 429.

Marglin, S. (1982), 'Knowledge and Power', paper presented at the SSRC Conference on Economics and Work Organization, York, March.

Marglin, S. (1984), 'Growth, Distribution and Inflation: a Centennial Synthesis', *Cambridge Journal of Economics*, 8.

Marris, R. (1963), 'A Model of the Managerial Enterprise', *The Quarterly Journal of Economics*, Vol. LXXVII, May.

Marris, R. (1967), *The Economic Theory of Managerial Capitalism*, London, Macmillan.

Marris, R. and Mueller, D. C. (1980), 'The Corporation, Competition, and the Invisible Hand', *Journal of Economic Literature*, Vol. XVIII, March.

Marx, K. (1973), *Grundrisse*, Penguin Books.

Marx, K. (1954), *Capital*, Vol. I, Lawrence and Wishart, London.

Marx, K. (1959), *Capital*, Vol. III, Lawrence and Wishart, London.

Miliband, R. (1973), *The State in Capitalist Society*, Quartet Books, London.

Mills, C. W. (1959), *The Power Elite*, Galaxy Books, Oxford University Press.

Minns, R. (1981), *Pension Funds and British Capitalism: The Ownership and Control of Shareholdings*, London, Heinemann.

Minns, R. (1981a), 'A Comment on "Finance Capital and the Crisis in Britain"', *Capital and Class*, No. 14.

Minns, R. (1982), *Take Over the City: The Case for Public Ownership of Financial Institutions*, Pluto Press.

Modigliani, F. (1958), 'New Developments on the Oligopoly Front', *Journal of Political Economy*, June.

Modigliani, F. (1970), 'The Life Cycle Hypothesis of Saving and Inter-Country Differences in the Saving Ratio', in Eltis, W. *et al.* eds., *Induction Growth and Trade, Essays in Honour of Sir Roy Harrod*, Oxford University Press.

Modigliani, F. (1975), 'The Life Cycle Hypothesis of Saving Twenty Years Later', in Parkin, M. and Nobay, A., eds., *Contemporary Issues in Economics*, Proceedings of the Conference of the Association of University Teachers of Economics, Warwick, 1973.

Modigliani, F. and Tarantelli, E. (1975), 'The Consumption Function in a Developing Economy and the Italian Experience', *American Economic Review*, December.

Muellbauer, J. and Portes, R. (1978), 'Macroeconomic Models with Quantity Rationing', *Economic Journal*, December.

Munnell, A. (1976), 'Private Pensions and Saving: New Evidence', *Journal of Political Economy*, Vol. 84, 1013–32.

Murray, F. R. (1968), *Economic Aspects of Pensions: A Summary Report*, National Bureau of Economic Research, New York.

Nichols, W. A. T. (1969), *Ownership, Control and Ideology*, Allen and Unwin.

Nyman, S. and Silberstron, A. (1978), 'The Ownership and Control of Industry', *Oxford Economic Papers*, 30.

O'Connor, J. (1973), *The Final Crisis of the State*, St Martin's Press, New York.

Pasinetti, L. L. (1962), 'Rate of Profit and Income Distribution in Relation to the Rate of Economic Growth', *Review of Economic Studies*, Vol. 29, 103–20.

Pasinetti, L. L. (1983), 'Conditions of Existence of a Two Class Economy in the Kaldor and More General Models of Growth and Income Distribution', *Kyklos*, Vol. 36, 91–102.

Peek, J. (1983), 'Capital Gains and Personal Saving Behaviour', *Journal of Money, Credit and Banking*, February.

Pitelis, C. N. (1984), Corporate Control, Social Choice and Financial Capital Accumulation, Ph.D. Thesis, Department of Economics, University of Warwick.

Pitelis, C. N. (1985), 'The Effects of Life Assurance and Pension Funds on Other Savings: The Postwar U.K. Experience', *Bulletin of Economic Research*, September.

Pitelis, C. N. and Sugden, R. (1986), 'The Separation of Ownership and Control in the Theory of the Firm: A Reappraisal', *International Journal of Industrial Organization*, 4.

Price, W. R. and Chouraqui, J. C. (1983), 'Public Sector Deficits: Problems and Policy Implications', *OECD Economic Outlook Occasional Studies*, June.

Radice, H. (1975), *International Firms and Modern Imperialism*, Penguin Books.

Ricardo, D. (1973), *The Principles of Political Economy and Taxation*, Dent Dutton.

Rose, H. (1983), 'Occupational Pension Schemes – Economic Background and Issues', Bank of England Panel of Academic Consultants, Panel Paper No. 20, 5–20.

Rothschild, K. W. (1942), 'A Note on Advertising', *Economic Journal*, April.

Rowthorn, B. (1977), 'Inflation and Costs', *Marxism Today*, November.

Rowthorn, B. (1980), *Capitalism, Conflict and Inflation*, Lawrence and Wishart, London.

Rowthorn, B. (1981), 'Demand, Real Wages and Economic Growth', *Thames Papers in Political Economy*, Autumn.

Sawyer, M. C. (1979), *Theories of the Firm*, Weidenfeld and Nicolson, London.

Sawyer, M. C. (1982), *Macroeconomics in Question*, Wheatsheaf Books Ltd, Brighton, Sussex.

Sawyer, M. C. (1982a), 'On the Specification of Structure Performance Relationships', *European Economic Review*, 17.

Scott, J. (1985), *Corporations, Classes and Capitalism*, 2nd edition, London, Hutchinson.

126   References

Scott, J. and Hughes, M. (1976), 'Ownership and Control in a Satellite Economy: A Discussion from Scottish Data', *Sociology*, 10, I.

Sherman, H. (1979), 'A Marxist Theory of the Business Cycle', *Review of Radical Political Economics*, Spring.

Solow, R. M. (1967), 'The New Industrial State or Son of Affluence', *The Public Interest*, Fall.

Spence, M. (1977), 'Entry, Investment and Oligopolistic Pricing', *Bell Journal of Economics*, 8.

Stafford, B. (1983), 'The Class Struggle, the Multiplier and the Alternative Economic Strategy', *Socialist Economist Review*.

Steindl, J. (1952), *Maturity and Stagnation in American Capitalism*, Oxford University Press.

Steindl, J. (1982), 'The Role of Household Savings in the Modern Economy', *Banca Nazionale del Lavoro Quarterly Review*, March.

Stoneman, P. (1984), *Economic Analysis of Technological Change*, Oxford, Oxford University Press.

Stopford, J. M. and Dunning, J. (1983), *Multinational Company Performance and Global Trends*, Macmillan.

Sugden, R. (1985), 'Why Transnational Corporations?', University of Edinburgh, Discussion Paper.

Surrey, M. J. (1970), 'Personal Income and Consumers' Expenditure', in Hilton and Heathfield, D. K., eds., *The Econometric Study of the U.K.*

Swamy, S. (1968), 'A Dynamic Personal Savings Function and its Long Run Implications', *The Review of Economics and Statistics*, Vol. XLX, February, 111–16.

Sweezy, P. M. (1942), *The Theory of Capitalist Development*, Basil Blackwell, Oxford.

Sweezy, P. M. (1953), *The Present as History*, Modern Reader, New York.

Taylor, L. D. (1971), 'Saving out of Different Types of Income', *Brookings Papers of Economic Activity*, 2, 383–407.

Taylor, L. D. and Weiserbs, D. (1972), 'Advertising and the Aggregate Consumption Function', *American Economic Review*, September.

Thompson, G. (1977), 'The Relationship Between the Financial and the Industrial Sector in the United Kingdom Economy', *Economy and Society*, Vol. 6, No. 3, August.

Threadgold, R. A. (1978), 'Personal Savings: The Impact of Life Assurance and Pension Funds', Bank of England, Discussion Paper No. 1.

Tobin, J. (1980), *Asset Accumulation and Economic Activity*, Basil Blackwell, Oxford.

Townend, J. C. (1976), 'The Personal Saving Ratio, *Bank of England Quarterly Bulletin*, March.

Wallis, K. (1979), *Topics in Applied Econometrics*, Basil Blackwell, Oxford.

Weisskopf, T. D. (1979), 'Marxian Crisis Theory and the Rate of Profit in the Post-War U.S. Economy', *Cambridge Journal of Economics*, December.

Williamson, O. (1964), *Economics of Discretionary Behaviour: Managerial Objectives in the Theory of the Firm*, Kershaw.

Williamson, O. (1967), 'Hierarchical Control and Optimum Firm Size', *The Journal of Political Economy*, Vol. 75, No. 2, April.

Williamson, O. (1970), *Corporate Control and Business Behaviour*, Prentice Hall.

References

Williamson, O. (1981), 'The Modern Corporation, Origins, Evolution, Attributes', *Journal of Economic Literature*, XIX, December.

Wolff, D. R. (1978), 'Marxian Crisis Theory: Structure and Implications', *Review of Radical Political Economics*, Spring.

Wood, A. (1975), *A Theory of Profits*, Cambridge University Press, Cambridge.

Wright, M. and Coyne, J. (1985), *Management Buy-Outs*, Croom Helm.

Zabalza, A., Pissarides, C. A. and Piachaud, D. (1978), 'Social Security, Life Cycle Saving and Retirement', in Collard, D., Lecomber, R. and Slater, M., eds., *Income Distribution: the Limits to Redistribution*, John Wright and Sons Ltd.

Zeitlin, M. (1974), 'Corporate Ownership and Control: The Large Corporations and the Capitalist Class', *American Journal of Sociology*, 79.

Index

Index

DATE DUE

Printed in the United States
25943LVS00006B/183